Social Skills Training Manual

Social Skills Training Manual

Assessment, Programme Design, and Management of Training

Jill Wilkinson
Department of Sociology, University of Surrey

and

Sandra Canter
Department of Psychology, University of Surrey

John Wiley & Sons

Chichester · New York · Brisbane · Toronto · Singapore

Library of Congress Cataloging in Publication Data:

Wilkinson, Jill.
  Social skills training manual.

  Includes bibliographical references and index.
  1. Social skills—Study and teaching.
  I. Canter, Sandra. II. Title.
  HM299.W54   302'.07   81-12957   AACR2

  ISBN 0 471 10056 0 (cloth)
  ISBN 0 471 10067 6

British Library Cataloguing in Publication Data:

Wilkinson, Jill
  Social skills training manual.
  1. Interpersonal relations—Study and teaching
  2. Life skills—Study and teaching
  I. Title   II. Canter, Sandra
  302'.07   HM132

  ISBN 0 471 10056 0 (cloth)
  ISBN 0 471 10067 6 (paper)

Typeset in 10/12pt Oracle by Photo-Graphics, Yarcombe, Nr. Honiton, Devon
Printed and bound in the United States of America.

This manual is affectionately dedicated to Lily and Zoë

Contents

Preface

This manual is intended for all those professionals—nurses, teachers, psychologists, psychiatrists, occupational therapists, social workers, probation officers, etc. who are using or wish to use social skills training with the people they are trying to help. It is a practical guide to doing social skills training.

The impetus to write this manual came from a variety of sources, not least our experience in training people in social skills during the course of our clinical work, carefully recording our programmes and methods as we proceeded. This experience was broadened through the training of others from a wide variety of professional backgrounds and orientations. These people were hoping to use or were already using social skills training with different types of clients, such as prisoners, stammerers, psychiatric patients, and the mentally and physically handicapped in various types of settings. We had to respond to the difficulties many of these people were experiencing putting into practice with their particular clients what they had read in textbooks on social skills. These trainers' workshops highlighted for us the pitfalls of applying predesigned packaged programmes to unselected clients. Consequently, we became aware of the necessity to train professionals in the skills of assessing and identifying social skill difficulties and in designing programmes to meet the specific needs of their selected client population.

Social skills training has developed very rapidly in recent years, but its progress has been somewhat marred by over-enthusiasm. It has become a fashionable term used so loosely as to encompass most of human activity from eating with a knife and fork to loving, understanding and empathizing with others. Yet it has a more precise meaning and the methods used are both simple and clear. We believe if the methods are to be further developed and used to their best advantage, they should not be confused, as they have been, with a variety of other approaches and those using social skills training methods should be clear about what they are doing and for what purpose.

Although many trainers/therapists have found social skills training of value, the results of early research on its effectiveness were disappointing. This, together with the general misuse of the term and the unsophisticated nature of some programmes, has meant that the method has come in for considerable attack. Our feeling is that it is too early to draw any conclusions as to its effectiveness until it has been properly tried and tested. We are still in the process of developing social skills training as a tool for change and it should not be surprising that poorly designed programmes do not work. As our experience and sophistication with the methods increases, so the research results become more encouraging. Looking to the future, we would hope that such methods would be part of general education, an acknowledgement by society that social skills are learned and not acquired through some automatic process.

This manual then is aimed at helping the would-be social skills trainer to do a good job. We have concentrated on what we see as the three major activities involved in doing this job: assessing problems, designing programmes and managing and running them. We are aware, of course, that in presenting the subject in this practical manner we have been able to give only the briefest coverage to information on social behaviour itself and have not involved ourselves in theoretical debates on the nature of social interaction, the relative importance of cognitive, emotional and behavioural components of skills training, or a research literature review. This is not to say that we advocate an uncritical acceptance of the method. We see evaluation of programmes as important; we see the development of more sophisticated methods as essential. We have worked together in this field over a number of years and have maintained our enthusiasm and enjoyment in the subject. For us social skills training is a positive and enjoyable form of training and we hope this manual will enable trainers to do it more effectively.

A final word about our orientation. We have worked largely within the psychiatric field and there is therefore a bias toward this type of client in the examples we have given. However, we have attempted to remedy this where possible by examples from other fields of endeavour, particularly by presenting a number of other programmes developed for other groups. We do advocate, however, that the reader use these only as fodder for his own creative solutions to his particular client's needs.

We would like to thank our patients for encouraging our work and those who attended our workshops for sharpening our thinking. Special thanks go to Nadine Hunter who organizes us and our activities without fault and to those who kindly contributed the programmes included in this manual.

1 Social Skill and Social Skills Training

1.1 SOCIAL INTERACTION

Person to person communication is an essential part of human activity. Most people in their day-to-day lives experience a wide variety of inter-personal situations. At work people interact with workmates and colleagues, the boss or subordinates. For the practical aspects of living it is necessary to deal with shopkeepers, bank managers, doctors, social security officers and the milkman. There are also, of course, the important interactions involved in developing and maintaining friendships, and in chatting to neighbours and acquaintances. Finally, there are the more intimate relationships of family, close friends, girlfriends, boyfriends and lovers.

1.2 SOCIAL GOALS

People interact with others for a variety of purposes, and each person will have his own aims or goals in a situation. Some goals of social interaction may be explicit and clearly defined, such as being successful at an interview, or changing an article at a shop, and the interaction can be extrinsically rewarded by achieving the goal (i.e. by getting the job or a new article). However, in many situations the goal may be implicit and less apparent, such as chatting at lunch time with a workmate or colleague, or simply greeting a neighbour in the street. Here the rewards are intrinsic, a part of the interaction itself. Such rewards might include being satisfied, interested, relaxed or stimulated in the company of others, all of which may lead to feelings of worth and increased self-esteem. How successful a person is in achieving his goals through communication with others, and thus receiving reinforcement for his behaviour, will influence his subsequent actions in similar situations.

1.3 SOCIAL SKILL

Communication with others involves both giving messages to another person and receiving and interpreting messages from him. It is a continuous two-way process in which the response also acts as feedback as to the effect of the message. The interaction will depend not only on the goals and messages a person wishes to convey, but on the situation he is in, his own personality, past experiences, what he observes of the other person and the consequent impression he forms of him. The communication itself involves the verbal or semantic content of speech, the words and sentences used and, equally important, the non-verbal aspects of the interaction, such as posture, use of eyes, tone of voice and facial expression. Verbal and non-verbal behaviour are therefore the means by which people communicate with others and they constitute the basic elements of social skill.

1.4   ACQUISITION OF SOCIAL SKILLS

Social skills are gradually acquired. The particular skills learned will to some extent be determined by the culture a person lives in and the particular social group to which he belongs. The child learns by imitating others, and parents in particular provide important models on which a child bases his own behaviour. There are other models, e.g. school teachers, peers and relatives, whose behaviour he observes in a variety of settings and subsequently may imitate. Instruction is also an important part of learning. The child may be directly instructed in how to behave in a particular social situation such as sharing toys with a friend, or asking the shopkeeper to show him where the pencils are kept. He is encouraged and rewarded for appropriate behaviour and discouraged for inappropriate behaviour. As the child develops he acquires the cognitive ability to assess situations, to be sensitive to other people, to review possible courses of action and to decide on the one which seems appropriate to him. In turn, the feedback he receives from others will give him information on the accuracy of his interpretation of a situation and appropriateness of his response. This is an on-going process and may continue into and throughout adulthood.

1.5   IMPAIRMENT OF SOCIAL SKILLS

The learning of appropriate social behaviour may be impaired for a variety of reasons, including lack of adequate models or learning opportunities, or poor instruction. Physical illness and disability or emotional difficulties can also disrupt the learning process. Alternatively, social skills may have been acquired and subsequently become impaired by periods of emotional disturbance such as anxiety, depression, psychosis or prolonged institutionalization. A deficit in social skills can in turn lead to the development of further social or psychological problems (see Section 3.1).

1.6   ORIGINS AND DEVELOPMENT OF SOCIAL SKILLS TRAINING

Social skills training has been developed as a method of teaching, in a systematic way, the skills of social interaction. This training has its origins in behaviour therapy and social psychology. Behaviour therapy itself developed from the application of learning theory principles derived from experimental psychology and gained much of its impetus from the clinical work of Wolpe (1958). This approach differed from previous approaches in that it focused directly on behaviour rather than underlying psychological causes of distress. Therapy was therefore concerned with re-learning new behaviour as opposed to gaining insight and restructuring the personality.

Wolpe (1958, 1969) and Wolpe and Lazarus (1966) developed a variety of behavioural methods, including assertion training for treating patients who were anxious or extremely submissive in their work or social relationships. The techniques he employed in teaching assertive behaviour included behavioural rehearsal (role-play) and task assignment (homework). Assertion, originally meaning to stand up for one's rights, was defined by Wolpe more broadly as the 'proper expression of any emotion other than anxiety towards another person' (Wolpe, 1969). Interest in assertion training grew rapidly in the 1960s and the concept of assertiveness was gradually enlarged to include a wide range of social behaviours.

There have been a number of other important contributions from behaviour theory and therapy to the methods of social skills training. One of the most important concepts is that of reinforcement, i.e. that behaviour can be changed as a result of the consequences of that behaviour (Skinner, 1953). Positive reinforcement or reward following behaviour increases the probability of that behaviour occurring again, whereas no reinforcement or negative reinforcement is likely to diminish the behaviour. Another important concept, which has been emphasized by the social learning theorists, is that of modelling or imitation learning whereby complex responses are acquired through observing models performing them (Bandura, 1969).

Finally, various cognitive factors are currently considered to be relevant in producing cognitive and behavioural change. These include the way in which the person thinks about himself and his problems (Ellis, 1971; Meichenbaum, 1974; Beck, Rush, Shaw and Emery, 1980), his cognitive evaluative appraisal of the situation (Linehan, Goldfried and

Goldfried, 1979), and his ability to generate alternative solutions and evaluate possible outcomes of various strategies (Bandura, 1977; Goldfried and D'Zurilla, 1969).

The actual methods employed in social skills training are a combination of the above procedures and principles. They are instruction, modelling, behavioural rehearsal (role-play), reinforcement and homework assignments (see Chapter 4).

Increasingly, much of the content of social skills training, i.e. what is taught, is derived from the experimental work of social psychologists (e.g. Argyle, 1969, 1975; see Chapter 2). This work has been concerned with studying specific behaviour of individuals in social situations in order to identify the basic elements of social behaviour and the way in which they are used in interactions of various kinds. There is a growing body of knowledge about non-verbal aspects of communication and speech and conversation, as well as the rules and norms of behaviour determining the structure of situations. Social skills training programmes result from a synthesis of the findings of social psychologists with the training procedures developed by behavioural psychologists.

1.7   CURRENT STATUS OF SOCIAL SKILLS TRAINING

Social skills training has expanded rapidly over the last five years. It is now used as an important training procedure in a wide variety of settings with many different types of client populations, including psychiatric patients, the mentally and physically handicapped, young offenders, long-term prisoners and school and college students.

There are many different approaches to the design of social skills training programmes. There are those that are designed to give a general training in a wide range of social behaviours and situations, and such programmes vary in content according to the type of population for whom they are intended (Trower, Bryant and Argyle, 1978; Goldsmith and McFall, 1975; Spence and Spence, 1980). Other programmes are concerned with training specific behaviours, such as assertive behaviour to control the expression of aggression (Rimm, Hill, Brown and Stuart, 1974), or skills for specific types of situations such as job interviews (Barbee and Keil, 1973) or heterosocial situations (Curran, 1977). Many people, however, prefer to design programmes to meet the specific needs of their individual clients (Liberman, King, De Risi and McCann, 1975;

Rahaim, Lefebvre and Jenkins, 1980; Marzillier and Winter, 1978). Although these programmes vary in style and content, the common elements are that they all aim to change social behaviour and they all use similar methods of training to achieve this end.

1.8 CHANGING SOCIAL BEHAVIOUR

Social skills training is concerned with changing social behaviour. This method makes no direct attempt to change other aspects of the person's experience. However, as he becomes more socially skilled, changes in other dimensions may occur. He may become less anxious, less depressed, feel less inadequate and more confident as he becomes more effective in social communication.

If the aim of social skills training is to change behaviour towards a more skilful response, it is important to establish criteria for defining socially skilled behaviour. Argyris (1965, 1968) refers to social skill as those interpersonal behaviours that contribute to the individual's effectiveness as part of a large group of individuals. Libet and Lewinsohn (1973) define social skill as the 'complex ability both to emit behaviours which are positively or negatively reinforced, and not to emit behaviours which are punished or extinguished by others'. Hersen and Bellack (1977) state that 'the overriding factor is effectiveness of behaviour in social interactions. However, determination of effectiveness depends on the context of the interaction.' Trower, Bryant and Argyle (1978) conceptualize man as 'pursuing social and other goals, acting according to rules and monitoring his progress in the light of continuous feedback from the environment'.

From these definitions it would appear that behaviour is judged to be socially skilled within a particular social context. There will be some purpose or goal in the interaction and the behaviour will be rewarded by feedback or reinforcement from others. However, none of these descriptions defines a skilful response in terms of specific behaviour in a given situation. Attempts have been made by social psychologists to establish the norms of social interaction in terms of the non-verbal and verbal behaviour appropriate in communicating specific messages (Argyle, 1969). Other studies have attempted to establish what behaviours constitute a competent response (Eisler, Miller and Hersen, 1973; Goldsmith and McFall, 1975). However, how effective a person is will depend on what he wishes to achieve in the particular situation he is in. Behaviour considered appropriate in one situation may obviously be inappropriate in another. The individual also brings to the situation his own attitudes, values, beliefs, cognitive abilities and unique style of interacting. Finally, social skill must be seen within a particular cultural framework, and patterns of communication vary widely between cultures and within any one culture depending on factors such as age, sex, social class and education.

Clearly, there can be no absolute 'criteria' of social skill. Although in experimental settings it might be shown that certain behaviours are more likely to achieve a particular goal, a competent response is usually what people generally agree is appropriate for an individual in a particular situation. Similarly, there can be no universally 'correct' way of behaving in a situation, but a number of different approaches which may vary according to the individual. Thus, two people may behave quite differently in a similar situation, or indeed one person in two separate but similar situations, but both responses might be considered to be equally socially skilled.

The implications of these issues are extremely important. Social skills training misapplied can be used to coerce the individual into conforming to rigid, stereotyped patterns of behaviour. At its best it can be used to increase the client's behavioural repertoire and awareness of social situations and offer him a wide variety of behavioural alternatives from which he is free to choose as, and when, he so wishes.

2 Social Behaviour

The social skills trainer must be familiar with the elements of social behaviour as described in this chapter in order to assess social skill deficit and design and carry out social skills training programmes.

As we have seen, social interaction is a complex process involving not only the behaviour, but the thoughts, feelings, values and attitudes of those participating. In terms of social skills training, however, the primary concern is with the basic elements of behaviour, both non-verbal and verbal. For example, in a conversation a person uses words to communicate a particular message. His facial, body and vocal cues can act to emphasize or reinforce this, or they can give a completely different message. These non-verbal elements also give information about the emotional meaning of the interaction and indicate the nature of the relationship between the individuals concerned. As he is speaking the person observes and assesses the other's behavioural response to what he is saying. This information, together with the consequent response, influences the next communication and so on. Research in social psychology is gradually elucidating the important elements of this process (Mehrabian, 1972; Argyle, 1972, 1975).

Whilst research is increasing our knowledge about the use of non-verbal and verbal behaviour, this information can only be used as guidelines in the training of social skill. It is evident, as discussed in the previous chapter, that a large number of factors will affect social behaviour in terms of the particular messages conveyed, as well as the channels used to convey those messages. Cultural factors are of particular importance and much of the research and the content of this chapter is based on Western culture. Also, within a society factors such as race, class, age, sex and social status will considerably affect the form and content of social interaction and therefore the skills involved. Moreover, people develop individual styles of interacting which become intrinsic to their personality and self-image. It is essential therefore when applying the following information in a training situation to be sensitive to the possible variations and exceptions that exist.

2.1 NON-VERBAL BEHAVIOUR

Non-verbal communication is unavoidable in the presence of other people. A person may decide not to speak, or be unable to communicate verbally, but he still gives messages about himself to others through his face and body. He is usually less aware of his non-verbal communication than of the verbal content of his speech. Non-verbal messages are also often received unawares. People form impressions of others from their non-verbal behaviour without identifying what it is about the person that is likeable or irritating, unless of course the behaviour is gross and easily identifiable.

Non-verbal messages have various functions. They can *replace* words altogether as when a parent quietens a child by a threatening glance or a person adopts a mode of dress that expresses rebellion. They can *repeat* what is spoken such as waving and saying goodbye. Importantly, they can *emphasize* a verbal message particularly of the emotional type: the clenched fist, wide eyes and loud voice adds strength to angry words. Non-verbal cues also *regulate* interaction. In conversation a person will signal to the other by a nod or a look that it is his turn to speak. Similarly, in a co-operative work situation a person may receive a gesture or head nod indicating his turn to take over the work task. Finally, the non-verbal message can *contradict* the verbal message. This is rarely done intentionally but the facial expression or a movement of the hands can reveal the true feelings which may be denied in the verbal content of the message. A common example is a person's reply to the question 'How are you?'. He may say he is fine, though his face reveals a state of apparent unhappiness (Mehrabian, 1971; Ekman and Friesen, 1969).

The following subsections give the elements of non-verbal behaviour.

2.1.1 Facial expression

Facial expression, with its visible mobility and flexibility, is the most important means of communicating non-verbally (Ekman, Friesen and Ellsworth, 1972; Ekman and Friesen, 1975). The face can communicate, for example, the degree of liking or understanding of, interest or involvement in, a person or situation. It expresses emotional states ranging from happiness to despair. Feelings are often reflected in the face even when the person wishes to disguise them. The face can respond instantaneously and is the most effective way to provide feedback to another person. For example, showing surprise and interest by raised eyebrows, or disapproval by a frown or tightened lips. Typical or idiosyncratic expressions also convey information about personality and identity.

2.1.2 Gaze

Eye gaze indicates that we are attending to others and is used in the perception of non-verbal signals of others. It is used to open and close communication channels and is particularly important in regulating and managing speaking turns (Kendon, 1967; Argyle and Cook, 1976). A period of eye contact often starts an interaction during which the listener usually looks at the speaker whose gaze may be averted a good deal of the time while speaking. The speaker will meet the gaze of the listener both to check that he is attentive and also to signify his turn to speak. Gaze can also be used to express emotions and attitudes. A strong gaze may indicate dominance or aggression and a person with little eye contact is usually seen as submissive or shy (Strongman and Champness, 1968). Eye contact is a common means of expressing affiliation and more intimate relationships. Gaze aversion may reflect, or be interpreted as, an unwillingness to interact.

2.1.3 Posture and gait

The position of the body and limbs, the way a person sits, stands and walks reflects his attitude and feelings about himself and his relationship to others (Mehrabian, 1972). Posture can reveal warmth, congruence with others, and the status and power in relation to the other. People may adopt different postures to those they like and dislike (Mehrabian, 1968). Leaning towards a person may show positive feelings toward him, whereas turning away may be an attempt to distance oneself. High status people tend to adopt more relaxed postures in the presence of junior people, who are likely to maintain a more formal sitting position in this situation (Mehrabian, 1968).

Posture and gait may also reflect a person's emotional state, particularly the degree of intensity and whether it is positive or negative (Ekman and Friesen, 1967). A message of anger can be emphasized when a person becomes tense and rigid, put his hands on hips and stamps his foot. Certainly, people use information from the position of a person's body to form impressions of them. A person who enters a room walking slowly with hunched shoulders may be thought of as timid, whereas the straight back and purposeful gait may convey a message of confidence. Individuals of course also have their own characteristic styles of posture and gait which reflect their personalities and self-image.

2.1.4   Gesture

Hand gestures have been found to be second in importance to facial cues as a means of non-verbal communication (Argyle, 1969). They sometimes are the only means of communication, as when attempting to communicate with someone whose language we do not speak. Gestures without words are used in other situations, such as directing a person to sit or stand, waving when greeting someone at a distance or warding off an attacker. Gestures also reinforce verbal messages, as when shaking a fist when shouting angrily, or showing the shape of something with the hands as it is being spoken about. Information about feelings can be leaked by 'redundant' movements. Scratching the face or picking at clothes can indicate anxiety or even impatience, although they may simply be idiosyncratic habits (Ekman and Friesen, 1967).

2.1.5   Proximity

How near, or far, high or low, people are in relation to others are all aspects of personal distance. People communicate their degree of liking, of intimacy and of differential role status through distance. A distinction has been made between intimate (0-18 inches), personal (18 inches-4 feet), social (4 feet-12 feet) and public distance (12 feet or more) (Hall, 1966). The form of a relationship and type of information exchanged at these distances will vary enormously from intimate exchange of confidences, through exchange of personal but less confidential material to impersonal business or social exchange. Interpersonal communication becomes impracticable at a public distance. The quality of an interaction may also be affected by the spatial relationship between the participants of an interaction, whether they are standing, or sitting, or one seated and the other standing.

There are also important individual differences, some people seeming to require a greater space between them than others (Porter, Argyle and Salter, 1970). This may be determined by factors such as height, a tall person requiring to stand further away from a shorter person in order to gain comfortable eye contact. Cultural factors and social conventions are important controllers of distance. For instance, it may be possible for people to tolerate and enjoy being closer at a party than in an office situation, and people usually unconsciously adjust the distances between them in order to feel more comfortable.

2.1.6 Touch

This is the earliest form of communication in infancy and important throughout life for expressing affiliative, sexual and aggressive feelings. Holding, caressing and stroking occur in nurturing, sexual and friendly relationships, and the amount and type of contact tends to vary with the degree of intimacy between those involved. Touch in these situations is used to communicate warmth, caring, love and affection as well as to signal emotional states such as fear, distress and exuberance. Touch is also used to express aggression by hitting, pushing or punching another person. More ritualized touching is a part of greetings and farewells, e.g. shaking hands or kissing cheeks. It may or may not have any emotional significance in such situations depending on the relationship of the people involved. Touch is also used to direct and instruct others, to steer a person by the elbow to a chair or guide his body in a particular action when teaching a motor skill.

There are enormous cultural variations both in the type and amount of touch used, and within a society the norms will vary for different groups (Argyle, 1969). Individuals in any one group will also vary in the amount of touching they personally will tolerate or enjoy. Play in young children involves a great deal of bodily contact but this decreases with age. Nurturant touching has to some extent become confused with sexual touching and physical contact between adults is uncommon in Britain compared to other countries (Jourard, 1966). However, the use of touch in friendship has been shown to be extremely socially rewarding for both giver and receiver (Mehrabian, 1972).

2.1.7 Personal appearance

Personal appearance not only affects our self-image but also our behaviour and the behaviour of people around us. Styles of dress, hair, cosmetics and jewellery provide a basis for first and sometimes long-lasting impressions (Walster, Aronson, Abrahams and Rottman, 1966). They convey messages about social status, personality, attitudes and emotional states (Kefgen and Touchie-Specht, 1971). Formal or informal dress may be chosen depending on the situation, the impression a person wishes to create and the way he wishes to feel. Thus, he may wear a pair of jeans and a sweater to go to a party and a suit and shirt to address a gathering or attend an interview. Appearance serves to differentiate between people: the old from the young, the formal from the informal, and between those with different social roles, the doctor and the patient, the judge and the accused.

2.1.8 Vocal cues

Vocal cues are concerned not with the content of speech but the way in which the words are spoken. They include emotional tone, pitch, volume, clarity, speed, emphasis and fluency, the ums and ers, pauses and hesitations. Vocal cues can drastically affect the meaning of what is said and how the message is received. The same sentence spoken in various tones of voice, or with particular words emphasized, etc. can convey very different meanings. I love you, can be said affectionately, teasingly, ironically or cruelly. The message conveyed in the words themselves can be less important and even contradicted by the tone of voice in which it is spoken (Ekman and Friesen, 1969). Voice cues particularly convey emotional states, although different people express the same emotions in various ways (Argyle, 1969). However, people who are anxious tend to talk more slowly, stutter, are repetitious and incoherent, while anger is usually expressed by a high-pitched, strong, loud voice (Eldred and Price, 1958; Cook, 1969). People also form judgements of others from their voice cues. Those people with a variety of voice pitch are likely to be judged as dynamic and extraverted and those with slow, flat speech as sluggish, cold and withdrawn. A person with a nasal voice is often perceived as unattractive, lethargic and foolish (Addington, 1968).

These non-verbal elements are rarely used in isolation. The meaning conveyed is usually a result of a combination of cues together with verbal behaviour and is assessed within a given context or situation. Non-verbal behaviour is sometimes wrongly learned or inappropriately used and, as a result, an attitude can be conveyed which is misleading or damaging to a social interaction. It is possible to improve skills in both sending and receiving non-verbal messages in order to be more expressive and increase sensitivity to others and thus communicate more effectively in social and interpersonal situations.

2.2 VERBAL BEHAVIOUR

Speech is used for a variety of purposes, for example to communicate ideas, to describe feelings, to reason and argue. The words used will depend on the situation a person is in, his role in that situation, the topic under discussion and what he is trying to achieve (Ervin-Tripp, 1973).

Situations vary from the intimate informal ones, such as friends talking over coffee at home, to the more formal ones, such as a discussion between an employer and employee at work. They will vary in terms of the range and amount of speech acceptable in those situations; a discussion with the boss at work is likely to be more restrictive than talking over coffee at home. The role a person is in will also be a determining factor, whether teacher, pupil, boss, worker or friend. In addition, each person brings to the situation his own personal style in terms of, for instance, how much he generally speaks or the characteristic phrases he uses.

The topic or content of speech of course, also varies. It can be highly personal, as between lovers or a mother and child, or impersonal, as between a shopkeeper and shopper. It can be concrete, as when giving directions to a particular building or describing a new dress, or abstract, as when discussing the relative merits of different political systems, or the meaning of happiness. It can be about matters internal to the speaker, his thoughts, feelings, attitudes and opinions, or external affairs, such as the organization of the office. It can vary in subject matter from the weather, gossip, family affairs or the latest car, to politics, religion and philosophy.

2.2.1 Elements of speech

Speech in interpersonal communication can be used to impart *information* to others about external factual matters or about more personal matters, opinions and attitudes. *Comments* are used to express agreement, disagreement, liking or disliking on matters being discussed or activities around. *Questions* are asked and *requests* made for information, services, goods or social responses. Speech is also used to *instruct* others in what to do, ranging from giving commands and directions to making tentative suggestions, and is an integral part of co-operative work whether in the classroom or at the work-bench. These different types of speech function to produce reactions in others through answers to questions, complying with requests, following instructions or enlarging on information. There is, however, the *expressive monologue* in which the speaker speaks for himself regardless of the effect he is having on others.

2.2.2 Conversation skills

The main form of interpersonal verbal communication is conversation. This may be brief or extended, be concerned with problem-solving, instructing, conveying information to others or simply with enjoying and sustaining social interaction. A conversation can be broken down into a number of processes, which are discussed below. It is important to remember that conversation does not consist of speech alone but includes the use of the non-verbal signals previously described.

2.2.2.1 Basic elements of conversation

Listening

Listening is important in order both to understand and to communicate interest in and feelings about what the other is saying (Barker, 1971). It is the way of providing feedback to the speaker who needs to know how his messages are being received, whether he is being clear, understood and accepted (Tustin, 1966; Leavitt and Mueller, 1968). Effective listening provides the speaker with necessary reinforcement for him to continue the conversation. Non-verbal skills are particularly important in listening; eye contact, facial expression, the raising of an eyebrow and the nod of the head. The verbal aspects include sounds or isolated words of agreement and encouragement or a comment on the events, feelings and mood the person is expressing, e.g. 'That sounds exciting' and 'That must have been awful'.

Talking

Everyone has experience, feelings and knowledge of various kinds, and this is what is exchanged in conversation. Much of conversation is about everyday matters and people often talk about things they have done or are involved in. Conversations often start with factual information and general statements, e.g. 'I went away last weekend', which are followed by specific statements giving details of what was done, seen, etc. For example, 'We stayed with an old friend and visited the local sights.' It then moves on to include the expression of feelings, attitudes and opinions about what is being described: 'It felt really good to get away and relax for a while.' Conversely, the other person can be encouraged to talk by asking questions that can be general, specific or about feelings or attitudes. Open questions rather than closed questions encourage the other to elaborate rather than giving single word replies, e.g. 'Did you go to the match at the weekend?', demands only a yes or no reply, whereas 'What did you do at the weekend?' demands a lengthier or more elaborate response.

2.2.2.2 Conversational sequence

Opening a conversation

There are a number of different ways of starting a conversation that are conventional and will vary according to the situation and whether the people involved are acquainted or not.

For example

1. Asking a question or making a request, e.g.
     'Do you know what time it is please?'
     'Where's a good place to eat around here?'

2. Comments about the environment, e.g.
     'It's cold in here today.'
     'I've never seen this shop so full….'
     'They seem to have painted this pub since I was here last.'

3. Greetings, e.g.
     'Hello, how are you?'
     'Hi, what have you been doing?'

4. Exchanging names, information about place of living, occupation, marital status, social contacts, e.g.
     'Hello, I'm Ron, what's your name?'
     'Good morning, I'm Mr Jones from the record department….

5. Personal questions or remarks, e.g.
     'You look good today.'
     'I like your hair.'

Maintaining a conversation

How the conversation proceeds will clearly depend upon the type of opening sequence. The conversation will continue by a question, a comment or the giving of information which may or may not be related to the opening remarks. A number of topics may be briefly explored before settling on one of mutual interest or a particular topic may be explored at a deeper level. In maintaining a conversation it is important that it does not become disjointed by a person talking about something completely different in response to the partner. A person can be embarrassed and hurt and the other considered rude if a topic is not taken up. In order to keep a conversation going and flowing smoothly, it is necessary to respond appropriately to the theme of the conversation by imparting some further information, disclosing feelings or asking a relevant question. Having explored one topic area a link statement can be used in changing to another subject, e.g. 'Talking of going to the match on Saturday reminds me I have to get the car fixed by then, there's something wrong with the radiator.' This might be followed by a discussion of car maintenance opened by a question such as: 'Do you know anything about radiators?' Changing the subject might also be done quite openly and blatantly by saying 'I know this has nothing to do with what we are talking about but....' This would be appropriate only at a suitable pause in the conversation.

Taking turns in speaking and listening is also important in developing and maintaining a conversation (Duncan, 1972). This involves paying careful attention to the non-verbal behaviour of others. The other will signal when he is ready to hand over the conversation by eye contact and inflection of voice as well as by the content, e.g. asking a question (Duncan and Fiske, 1977). He may also be responding to the non-verbal signal of the listener who will have indicated through eye contact, facial expression and posture that he wishes to speak (Kendon, 1973). In any satisfying conversation taking turns operates by mutual agreement but may not involve all parties making equal contributions. By careful timing, constant interruptions or prolonged silences are avoided.

Ending a conversation

When ending a conversation and leaving the situation people usually signal their readiness to leave non-verbally as well as verbally, e.g. they might sit forward in the chair in readiness to stand up, get out car keys, withdraw gaze and use a phrase such as 'I must go now because....' The statement may also include an indication of further contact, e.g. 'I'll see you tomorrow', accompanied by parting looks, a smile and movement away. Many people develop their own individual routines for partings such as 'Bye, see you soon'. When not actually leaving the situation it is usual to signal that the conversation has ended by withdrawing eye contact and engaging in some other activity. This may or may not be accompanied by a remark such as 'I must get on with…'.

2.3   ASSERTIVE BEHAVIOUR

Assertive behaviour has been defined as 'behaviour which enables a person to act in his own interests, stand up for himself without due anxiety, and to express his rights without denying the rights of others' (Alberti and Emmons, 1974). Lazarus (1973) proposed a broader definition, suggesting that assertive behaviour be divided into four separate categories: the ability to say 'no'; the ability to ask for favours or make requests; the ability to express positive and negative feelings; and the ability to initiate, continue and terminate general conversation. In this sense, assertive behaviour is almost synonymous with the term 'social skill'. In this manual the term 'assertion' is being used more specifically to cover all areas of self-expression which is similar to the definition of Wolpe who refers to assertion as 'the proper expression of any emotion other than anxiety towards another person' (Wolpe, 1969). Self-expression includes the ability to communicate feelings to others, to express friendship and affection, annoyance and anger, joy and pleasure, grief and sadness, and to both give and accept praise and criticism.

When being non-assertive a person denies his needs and fails to express his feelings. He may be unable to say no to an unreasonable request, to ask someone to do something for him, to defend himself against accusation, or to tell someone how he feels about them. Assertion is not simply dealing with negative situations but is rather a style which may influence many social interactions. Being assertive does not mean being aggressive. Aggression may be the individual's only response in situations where he needs to stand up for himself or make his needs known, and the aggressive person may therefore need to learn to be assertive rather than aggressive in these situations.

There are many situations in which assertive behaviour would be appropriate, and the examples in the following subsections are just a few of the situations which many clients report having difficulty with and which are often included in training programmes.

2.3.1   Standing up for your rights/not being cheated

In a situation where a person has, for example, been deliberately sold a defective article, such as a bag of apples, some of which are rotten, it is important to make a quick assessment of the situation and confront the seller without apologizing, using a firm, polite and steady voice, looking him clearly in the eye: 'Excuse me, do you realize two of the apples in this bag are rotten.' If the person tries to get out of the situation, the assertion should be made firmer' 'These apples are rotten, would you please change them.' (It is of course useful to know your legal rights in any situation and this can be resorted to if all else fails.)

2.3.2   Making a request/asking someone out

In asking someone out it is important to be direct and positive without embarrassment, making the message as clear as possible. Eye contact, facial expression and tone of voice are particularly important here. It may be useful to sound out the person first before making the actual request, e.g. 'I sometimes go to the pictures, would you like to go some time?' The reply will give some indication as to whether or not to proceed with a direct request: 'Do you want to come to the Odeon with me on Saturday night?'

2.3.3   Coping with refusal

Having asked a person out there is always the possibility that they may refuse. In this case it is important to recover from the situation and although feeling disappointed to feel that the situation has been handled well. This can be done by making a face-saving statement, e.g.
    'Do you want to come to the Odeon on Saturday night?'
    'No, I don't feel like it.'
    'Oh well, some other time then.'

2.3.4   Refusing a request

In saying no to another's request a judgement as to the reasonableness of the request has to be made. If it is a reasonable request, e.g. being asked out on a date by a friend, the refusal will often be accompanied by an excuse: 'I am sorry, I can't, I have to look after my sister's baby tonight.' If the request is unreasonable, an acknowledgement of the person's needs, accompanied by a definite no without a justifying account is necessary, e.g. 'I realize you would like me to stay in tonight, but no I can't.' If the person persists with the request, it is important to point this out, e.g. 'I've said no, don't go on about it.'

2.3.5   Showing appreciation

Paying compliments is one way of showing appreciation for a person or expressing positive feelings toward another. These might be about a person's appearance, e.g. 'You're looking attractive today', or about aspects of his personality or behaviour or things he has achieved, e.g. 'What a super meal you cooked today.' It is important to convey warmth through tone of voice, eye contact and facial expression.

2.3.6   Making apologies

Being able to apologize is very necessary since people inevitably find themselves in situations where they have either made a mistake or where things have gone wrong. These are situations which, because they are difficult to handle, are sometimes avoided, e.g. a person has invited a friend round to his house and has forgotten and gone out. The following day he sees the person at work. When apologizing it is always desirable to make the approach first if possible and to state clearly and firmly with direct eye contact the apology. 'Look, I really am very sorry about last night. I completely forgot.' It is then necessary to make good the situation, maybe in this case by repeating the invitation: 'I would like you to come, can you make it tomorrow evening?'

This chapter has been concerned with the basic elements and forms of social interaction. Many social situations are of course more complex than those described here but nevertheless will involve the application of the basic skills. In social skills training those complex situations can be broken down, discussed and strategies for dealing with them practised and learned.

These might include such interactions as:

(a) forming and maintaining friendships with people of the same or opposite sex,
(b) job interviews,
(c) dealing with a dominant member of the family,
(d) dealing with authority figures or professionals,
(e) taking a leadership role, as in a work situation.

3 Assessment for Social Skills Training

3.1   POOR SOCIAL FUNCTIONING: IDENTIFYING A CLIENT POPULATION FOR SOCIAL SKILLS TRAINING

As yet, little has been established regarding the factors that determine the development and appropriate performance of social behaviour, and consequently the reasons for deficiencies in social skills. However, it would seem reasonable to accept that social behaviour is learned and that a number of disruptions can occur in both learning and performance. The person may never have acquired the skills necessary for making satisfactory social relationships or dealing with a wide variety of situations. Failure to learn these skills may derive from a number of circumstances. The person's interpersonal environments may not have been instructive; parents as models for the child may have been deficient, idiosyncratic or non-existent; there may have been conflicts between social requirements and parental reinforcements; or skills may have been acquired in a restricted range of environments, either because of lack of opportunity or emotional factors such as anxiety or embarrassment leading to the avoidance of those situations.

Failure to learn social skills can lead to isolation, loneliness, rejection, poor self-image, low self-esteem and may be an antecedent to a wide range of psychological problems and disturbances of behaviour. People can present with anxiety, depression, sexual problems, aggressive behaviour, delinquency, etc. or simply complain of an inability to get on with people, shyness or loneliness.

Poor social functioning can also arise as a consequence of other problems of a psychological, physical, social or organic origin, which may affect all areas of behaviour, including social behaviour. Extreme anxiety, depression, schizophrenia, mental and physical handicaps can all be associated with problems in social behaviour, the learning of which may have been disrupted as a consequence of these other problems. In some cases it may be that social behaviour has been acquired, but the individual is temporarily unable to engage in social activity because of other emotional or physical problems. The depressed person may avoid social contact which in itself may deepen the depression. The stroke patient may have lost confidence and be having difficulty adjusting to his changed physical status. Finally, a prolonged stay in an institution such as a hospital or prison can affect the social behaviour of the individuals in them. Institutions often provide a very restricted learning environment, as well as developing a social culture unique to themselves and unrelated to a wider social context.

The extent of any individual's deficit can vary. It may involve a particular behaviour such as eye contact or include every aspect of social behaviour, verbal and non-verbal. The difficulty may occur in a wide variety of settings or be limited to certain situations, such as those with authority figures or members of the opposite sex. As illustrated in the case examples given (Figure 1), the clinical diagnosis or label assigned to the individual can be varied. Whatever this might be, it is important that the problems in social functioning are recognized so that the appropriate training can be given. It may be necessary, with some individuals, to work with other aspects of his problem, thus necessitating the use of other methods. However, there will be people for whom social skills training alone may lead to the alleviation of other problems consequent on the social skill deficit.

Whether the social skills deficit is seen as a cause or a result of some other problem is in practice often difficult to determine. What is most important is to establish a thorough and comprehensive definition of the person's problem or problems so that suitable treatment and training strategies can be adopted. The social skills deficit needs to be carefully assessed and considered in relation to any other problems the individual may be experiencing.

3.2 REFERRAL AND SELECTION OF CLIENTS FOR SOCIAL SKILLS ASSESSMENT

How the client is selected for social skills assessment will depend on the organizational structure and the role of the therapist/trainer. If the client has been referred by someone else, it will be necessary to carry out a fairly detailed general assessment before focusing on the social skills problems. Where the therapist already knows his client well and has already conducted, or been present at, a general assessment interview, he might proceed straight to the detailed assessment of social skill.

It is important to establish and maintain a good working relationship with referring agents, specifying the type of problems for which social skills training is useful. Feedback from the assessment should be given and if training is not thought to be suitable, the reasons should be stated and possible alternatives suggested. In this way the referring agency learns which clients are more likely to benefit from social skills training.

EXAMPLES OF CLIENTS WITH SOCIAL SKILL PROBLEMS

John B. is 25 years old. He lost both legs in a car accident and suffered minimal brain damage resulting in some loss of speech fluency and is confined to a wheel chair for a good part of the day. He was always a sociable person finding relationships with others easy and pleasant. Since the accident he has become withdrawn and is embarrassed and unwilling to meet with other people, including his former friends. He finds asking for and receiving help particularly difficult.

Jane T. is 17 years old. She originally presented with depression and agoraphobia. She left school 8 months ago and has been unemployed since that time. At school she was excessively shy, made no friends and was unable to respond in class when asked questions. She was a severe school refuser and consequently, though quite bright, has a poor academic record. She finds the thought of job interviews and the prospect of going to work terrifying and rarely goes out of the house.

Terry S. is 28 years old and has worked successfully in a bank since leaving school. He has always had an active social life with many friends with whom he has been a popular figure. At work he related well to his immediate colleagues and had been making steady probress in his career. Ten months ago he was promoted to assistant manager and within three weeks he lost his voice at work. This symptom, for which no physical basis was established, continued and a diagnosis of hysterical aphonia was made. There is some fluctuation in his voice volume from being completely unable to make a sound to low volume speech. The condition seems to be exacerbated when he is required to use his authority in interpersonal situations at work.

Figure 1.

Mary J. is 25 years old. She is mentally handicapped and has been living in an institutionalized environment since she was six months old. Her speech is good and she communicates well with other patients and staff in the hostel where she lives. However, on outings she tends to approach strangers, particularly men, offering sweets and asking them personal question to seek reassurance of her attractiveness. This frequently causes embarrassment to others and creates a situation where she is rejected.

Kevin S. is 29 years old. He has been released from prison after serving a six months' sentence for assault. He has always had difficulty in getting on with people and appears surly and aggressive. Although he has been married and now has a girlfriend, he finds it impossible to show any positive feelings in close relationships. Currently he has a job in a warehouse but he keeps very much to himself and has difficulty in taking orders in his job. He is afraid that he will become aggressive and the previous pattern will be repeated, resulting in him ending up in prison again.

Jo B. is 40. He has been a hospitalized psychiatric patient for fifteen years and is diagnosed schizophrenic. He is now taking part in a rehabilitation programme and is due to go to a group home in three months' time. He has no difficulty with the practical aspects of living such as cooking, etc. and responds well when spoken to, but has not been seen to initiate contact with others. He himself complains of loneliness, has no friends on the ward but gets on well with the staff. His appearance is scruffy and unkempt and he walks with a stoop.

3.3   PURPOSE OF ASSESSMENT OF SOCIAL SKILL

The client's social skill needs to be assessed for the following reasons

(a) To specify the social skills assets and deficits of the prospective client.
(b) To assess the client's motivation for change.
(c) To decide whether social skills training is the most suitable form of training/therapy.
(d) To give information about social skills training.
(e) To identify and set training goals.
(f) To design the programme.
(g) To monitor the progress of the client.
(h) To evaluate the effectiveness of the programme.

Systematic assessment is one of the most important factors in social skills training. The success or failure of any training programme may ultimately depend upon careful assessment. It is important that clients are not allocated randomly to social skills groups, but that training programmes are designed to meet the particular needs of the client or groups of clients. This requires careful and detailed assessment throughout the training.

3.4   METHODS OF ASSESSMENT

3.4.1   The assessment interview

A focused interview offers a very good way of eliciting social and interactional data from individuals who are able to report on their behaviour with reasonable accuracy. As is true of all clinical interviews, those which focus on the person's behaviour with others depends on establishing a good rapport. The atmosphere should be relaxed and friendly and the interviewer, whilst concentrating on actual behaviour, should be sensitive to the person as a whole.

Some thought should be given beforehand to the environment and seating arrangements. Chairs should, if possible, be of the same height and placed at a distance and angle to assist, rather than hinder, the interaction. There should, if possible, be no interruptions.

As well as preparing the environment, the trainer should be prepared himself. Is he clear about the purpose of the interview? Does he have all the necessary data from previous interviews? Is he clear what information he requires and what he needs to impart? If he is interviewing with a co-trainer, who is going to ask what questions?

Having prepared the setting and himself, the trainer can now proceed with the interview. He should first welcome the client and then explain to him the purpose of the interview, making sure that the client has understood.

Then he will want to obtain detailed information about the person's interpersonal and social relationships, and difficulties in social situations. What are the problems? In which situations do they occur? What actually happens? How does the individual behave in these situations? How do others respond to him? Who are the people involved? How often does it occur?

For example:
What is the problem?
   'I have a terrible stutter and I can't go to school.'
In which situations?
   'When I'm asked a question in class.'
What actually happens?
   'I think I know the answer and start talking and then get all muddled up and start stuttering and waving my arms about and then my mind goes blank.'
What happens next?
   'Sometimes I just sit down and feel awful and last week I ran out of the room.'
Who are the people involved?
   'Well — it happens with all the teachers but it's worse with one particular one.'
How often?
   'Just about every day.'

Only in a small number of clients will the difficulty be restricted to one situation and all the situations should be explored in this way.

Frequently clients will talk initially about personal problems in terms of unhappiness, anxiety, depression, conflict, etc. rather than the ability or inability to handle social relationships. It is therefore important that the interviewer structures the interview around specific interpersonal relationships and situations. For example, a client may report 'anxiety' in interpersonal situations. This could mean a number of things:

For example
(1) he remains silent;
(2) he talks non-stop;
(3) he stutters and stammers a great deal;
(4) he smiles and giggles;
(5) his heart beats rapidly and he feels queazy; or
(6) he feels stupid and inadequate although he appears to perform adequately.

The interviewer should establish which of these reactions the client experiences and in what situations.

A client might report a general feeling of depression. She could then be asked about situations at work, at home or in her social life in order to elicit information about how she handles the interpersonal aspects of those situations and to identify areas of difficulty or avoidance.

The interviewer should always check carefully what the client means by the words and phrases he uses. They may both attribute different meanings to words and it is only by asking for details that the interviewer can get a clear idea of the nature and degree of the social deficits.

The emphasis of the interviewer will be on the difficulties which the client is experiencing, but it is important that the positive aspects of the client's social functioning are not ignored. What does he do well? What does he cope with adequately?

The interviewer will receive information on the client's performance not only from what he reports, but by observing his behaviour throughout the interview, e.g. the fluency and content of speech, the attitudes expressed, his posture, eye contact, etc. and this valuable source of material should not be overlooked.

Having obtained detailed information about the client's social functioning, the trainer will need to establish what changes the client would like to make, i.e. what he would like to achieve and the extent to which he is prepared to work towards making these changes (a detailed analysis of goals will be made later). It may be that there are factors in the client's environment which sustain the unskilled or maladaptive behaviour, e.g. a father seeing his son's violent behaviour as manly, anti-social behaviour being the criterion for acceptance in a peer group, a mother feeling needed by her unassertive daughter. It is therefore important to check out how the client thinks others would respond to changes in his behaviour and how he feels about this.

In some cases it may be necessary to spend time before or during training exploring this area in order that the positive changes brought about by training will not be negated in the home environment (see Section 6.4).

At this stage the trainer can put the information obtained from the interview together with that obtained by other assessment procedures (see following sections) and can formulate and feedback to the client how he sees the difficulty, checking out the accuracy of his perceptions and understanding. The trainer will, by this stage, have a reasonably good idea as to whether or not social skills training is suitable for the particular client and (possibly depending on the situation and resources available) whether individual or group training would be more appropriate (see Section 5.1). If training is not considered appropriate, the individual should be informed of this (not that **he** is not suitable for training), the reasons given, and if the interviewer is in the position to do so, alternative arrangements could be discussed, e.g. it is possible that systematic desensitization would be more appropriate than social skills training for social anxiety.

If social skills training is considered suitable, the interviewer should give the client some information about the training. At this stage it may not be necessary or desirable to go into great detail, but just to give an outline of the training in terms of length and number of sessions, whether it is to be in a group or not, and that it will involve active participation. Homework assignments can be mentioned at this stage but detailed preparation of the client can take place at a later stage (see Sections 4.6 and 6.1).

The trainer can then find out whether or not the client is interested in taking part in a social skills training programme and any questions can be answered. If the client does not think that training would be helpful and it is not for him, then the interviewer should try to find out the reasons for this. Is it because he is worried about going into a group? Most people are. Reassurance can be given that other members all have problems in getting on with people and probably feel the same way. Alternatively, a period of individual training may help. Is it because, when it comes down to it, he really doesn't want to make the changes? If this is the case, then social skills training as such probably won't help him. Is it because it all sounds like going back to school and a bit silly? The trainer probably has not done a good job of giving the rationale and explanation of training. He should try again.

If the client is undecided and would like more time to digest the information and possibly discuss it with family members, another appointment can be made.

3.4.2   Observation in the natural setting

Information can be obtained about the client's behaviour in his own environment by observing him in actual social interactions. This has to be done carefully and unobtrusively in order not to disrupt or change the behaviour being observed. It can be a useful method for collecting information particularly with clients who have difficulty reporting on their own behaviour.

Observation can be done formally or informally, by the trainer or by parents, friends or other staff members. Informal observation involves being with the client in his natural setting and reporting on how he behaves in a variety of situations. If the client is living at home, for example, a relative can be asked to observe and report on how the client copes with visitors, answering the telephone, shopping, making requests, general conversation, etc. As with the assessment interview, behavioural detail should be sought, i.e. what did the person say in the situation, how did he behave, his posture, eye contact, facial expression. In a residential setting, where the institution forms the 'home' environment, the behaviour can similarly be observed by the trainer or other members of staff. For example, they could be asked to observe and report on who the client talks to. Does he get on better with members of staff or with other patients. Does he initiate any interactions. Does he make requests, stand up for himself, speak only when spoken to. Does he speak at all. What he does at meal-times and in other departments such as occupational therapy. What he does when listening to others.

This type of informal observation cannot be an objective assessment but only an account of how a person sees the other's behaviour, and this must be taken into consideration. The procedure can be improved by the use of observation scales designed to assess specific behaviours. This more formal observation procedure requires that the observers be trained in the use of the scales so that more accurate information can be obtained. A check list or rating scale can be devised that should specify the behaviours which are to be observed. For example, a check list might be made up of a list of behaviours such as making a greeting, opening a conversation, listening, making requests, etc. which the observer ticks off each time the client performs that particular response during a given period of time. In this way the trainer can collect information on how frequently certain behaviours occur. Rating scales can also be used which will give a subjective account of the quality of a response in terms of its appropriateness. In the example given, the observer is asked to rate particular behaviours of the client in a number of specified situations, giving a rating of between 1 and 5 for appropriateness and indicating the frequency of occurrence of other behaviours. These scores can provide a useful means of assessing change over time.

EXAMPLES OF RATING SCALES

Non-verbal behaviours (qualitative) — at the dinner table				
appropriate 5	4	3	2	inappropriate 1
Eye contact		√		
Facial expression		√		
Posture				√
Voice tone			√	
Voice volume			√	

Verbal behaviour (quantitative) — at the dinner table
frequency of behaviours
Starts conversation √ √ √
Maintains conversation √
Makes requests
Listens √ √ √ √ √
Asks questions

EXAMPLES OF SELF-REPORT MEASURES

Author	Scale	Behaviour measured	Population for whom it was designed
Bryant and Trower (1974)	Social Situations Questionnaire	Difficulty with a wide range of social situations	Adult college students
Watson and Friend (1969)	Social Avoidance and Distress Scale (SAD)	Distress, discomfort and anxiety in a wide variety of social situations	Adult college students
	Fear of Negative Evaluation (FNE)	Apprehension about social disapproval from others	
Goldsmith and McFall (1975)	Interpersonal Situation Inventory	Difficulty with a range of interpersonal situations	Male adult psychiatric patients
Rathus (1973)	Rathus Assertive Schedule	Assertive behaviour	Adult college students
Wolpe and Lazarus (1966)	Wolpe and Lazarus Assertiveness Scale	Assertive behaviour	Adult clinical population
Gambrill and Richey (1975)	Assertion Inventory	Assertive behaviour	Adult college students
Twentyman and McFall (1975)	Survey of Heterosexual Interactions	Heterosexual behaviour in males	Adult college males

3.4.3 Self-report measures

Self-report scales can of course only be used with those clients who are able to report on their behaviour in social situations and should not be used as a major source of information. Scales vary enormously in their scope, some being concerned with specific aspects of social behaviour, such as assertion, and some being of a more general nature. However, with any self-report measure, it is not justified to assume that it will cover all the problem areas of any individual client. Moreover, in answering questionnaires there is a tendency for people to present themselves in a good light. They will of course vary in the extent to which they are aware of their own behaviour in social situations and therefore the accuracy with which they can report it. If used carefully, however, they can aid in mapping out broad problem areas which can then be defined more precisely in an assessment interview. They do have the advantage of being economical in time and can be scored objectively. Therefore they can be used to compare individual problems and the same individual over time thereby providing a useful assessment of change. The list presented here provides examples of some of the scales which have been developed largely for research purposes with specific populations. The reader should consult the original articles for details on the reliability and validity of these measures.

3.4.4 Assessment using role-played scenes

A role-play can be set up as part of the assessment procedure. This can take the form of a standard social situation which the client is likely to encounter, or be based on a particular situation which the client has identified as difficult. Details of this situation should be sought and appropriate props supplied (tables, chairs, etc.) and role-models briefed (see Section 4.3). The client is instructed to behave as far as possible as he does in the real situation and at the end of the scene he should be asked how accurately his behaviour in role-play reflected his behaviour in the actual situation. If not at all, then further information about the situation should be sought and the scene role-played again. Once again, check lists and rating scales can be used to rate specific behaviours. Role-play can provide the trainer with behavioural information about which the client may be unaware or on which he is unable to report with accuracy. However, it should be noted that this form of assessment can only provide a rough estimate of what actually happens and should be used alongside the client's verbal report of that situation.

All or any combination of these procedures can be used for an initial assessment of the individual's difficulties and provide the basic information for goal-setting and programme design. They can also be used to monitor the progress of the individual during the training so that modifications to the training programme can be made if necessary.

3.5   GOAL-SETTING

The process of goal-setting would normally be done at a second interview with the client, once the information on which this is to be based is available. Prior to this, however, the training methods should be described to the client, and his agreement to participate in training obtained. Even in cases where little direct information has been obtained from the client himself, as with chronic institutionalized patients, it is important that he is consulted and informed about training, e.g. 'I've noticed that on the ward you always seem willing to answer when someone speaks to you or asks you something but I've never seen you start a conversation with anyone. We are going to run a course/training programme here and its aim is to help to get people talking to each other a bit more....'

The client should formulate his own goals aided by the trainer feeding back the assessment information to him. The goals should be realistic, i.e. within the client's capabilities, relevant to the individual's everyday situations and should be formulated in behavioural rather than general terms, e.g.

not 'To be happier at work', **but** 'To be able to chat to the other girls in the office and to allocate the work to them. To go into the boss's office confidently and take his work.'

not 'To be one of the gang' **but** 'To be able to make suggestions about what the gang should do and to say "no I don't want to" when that is the case.'

not 'To be more confident', **but** 'To enter a pub looking confident and to chat with the people at the bar.'

It is also necessary to list the goals in order of difficulty, as perceived by the client, so that programmes can be designed to proceed in stages from the easy to the more difficult areas.

All the general statements (I want to be happy, etc.) are of little or no help in designing social skills training programmes. However, they are undoubtedly very real goals for the client and may ultimately form the criteria by which the client judges the effectiveness or otherwise of training. None the less goals need to be detailed, specific and behavioural so that exercises can be designed to enable the client to attain his specified goals, thereby achieving his more general objective.

The degree to which a client can articulate his own goals will of course vary. Where the client has been in hospital or prison for a number of years he may, because of the process of institutionalization and probably having adopted the limited role of patient or prisoner, find it difficult to think in terms of goals and change. In this case the trainer might have to present to the client a range of possibilities and suggested goals from which to choose, depending upon the overall aim of the training, e.g. rehabilitation into the community, job finding, dealing with authority, and the particular difficulties of the individual concerned. Here the trainer must be guided by what would be realistic for his client given his limitations, particular interests, etc. Where a limited number of goals might have initially been set by the therapist, it is possible that with training the client will become aware of a wider range of possibilities for change and develop the skills to set his own goals.

In some instances the client's goals may conflict with those of the trainer. For example, the goals of a young offender might be to re-establish himself with his peer group of similar offenders by taking part in their activities. Where this is the case it would be advisable for the therapist to raise the issue with the client and possibly come to some agreement. If the client were able to communicate more effectively generally, his choice of acquaintances might be less restricted and he would have a wider population from whom to choose his associates. The therapist must be free to disagree with the values held by the client but, at the same time, he should avoid imposing his own goals on the client, although he will of course be influenced by the values he holds.

At this stage the trainer will have:

(a) detailed information about the client's problems, the social situations and relationships he has difficulty with and his specific behavioural deficits, verbal and non-verbal

(b) a list of the client's goals or behaviours he wishes to achieve, in order of difficulty.

This information provides the essential material for programme design (see Chapter 5).

3.6   EVALUATION OF SOCIAL SKILLS TRAINING PROGRAMMES

Assessment procedures can be administered before, during and after training to evaluate the effectiveness of a particular training programme. Of course, without the use of proper controls any changes reported or observed cannot be attributed to the training programme alone but may be due to the increased attention given or simply the passage of time. However, a simple pre and post assessment may give some indication to the trainer of the changes taking place.

In evaluating training it is necessary to predict what changes are expected in terms of the specific goals set for the individual and possibly the more minute aspects of his behaviour, e.g. increased use of eye contact. These can be assessed by using the procedures discussed, particularly role-play, rating scales, self-report measures and observation in the natural setting. There is now a large body of research literature and all these methods have been reported (Bellack and Hersen, 1980).

A thorough examination of the social skills method would involve a systematic research approach. There are many possible experimental designs but the most frequently used involve comparisons of groups receiving a variety of types of training or treatment or a comparison of a social skills group with a no-treatment or pseudo-training group (Trower, Yardly, Bryant and Shaw, 1978; Linehan, Goldfried and Goldfried, 1979). There are many such studies and that of Goldsmith and McFall (1975) provides an example. They assigned 36 male psychiatric patients to three groups: interpersonal skills training, pseudo-therapy control, and assessment-only control. For assessment before and after training they used a combination of self-report rating scales examining the client's expectations and degree of difficulty with a number of social situations. Post-training they also used two role-play assessments, in one the client had to respond to a variety of pre-selected interpersonal situations and in the other, hold a conversation with and make a request of a stranger.

Alternatively, single case studies have been conducted which involve training specified behaviours which are compared for change with behaviours that have not been trained (Rahaim, Lefebvre and Jenkins, 1980).

Marzillier and Winter (1978) used a multiple base line design in their single case studies of four psychiatric patients. They used a variety of procedures for assessment based on interviews, rating scales and role-play, and individual target behaviours were selected for training on the basis of a videotaped recording of a conversation with the therapist. This conversation was repeated at various intervals throughout training in order to monitor changes in target behaviours. One target behaviour was selected and trained and the effects of training assessed, a second behaviour was added, etc. until all target behaviours had been trained. This allowed for a schematic training of specified target behaviours in a sequential and cumulative fashion and a continuous evaluation of change.

Having established that change takes place, it is also important to establish if this change is maintained over time. This would necessitate following up all subjects and reassessing them at intervals. Most studies are inadequate in this respect having no follow up or following up, only at a short period after completion of treatment. Treatment studies that have included longer-term follow up of a year or more have shown that differences between treatment and no-treatment groups can disappear (Sloan, Staples, Cristol, Yorkston and Whipple, 1975). Long-term follow up data will also provide us with useful information on whether 'booster' training is necessary.

In order for social skills training to be considered effective, the behaviour learned in the training sessions must be shown to generalize to the person's interactions in real life situations. One might also expect generalization of learning to take place in other situations and with other people. Generalization across situations can be measured by including in the assessment situations for which no specific training has been given (Goldsmith and McFall, 1975). Generalization across people can be measured by including a second role-model with whom the client has had no contact at the pre-training assessment (Edelstein and Eisler, 1976).

Generalization to the real environment is more difficult to assess and is usually dependent upon the report of the client and of others with whom he has contact. Unobtrusive observation of the client in his own environment would be most effective. However, because of the ethical and practical difficulties in implementing this type of procedure most researchers have confined themselves to naturalistic observation in the hospital setting, using pre and post ratings of specified behaviours (Shepherd, 1977, 1978).

Although it is expected that social skills training will bring about changes in social behaviour, it is important to assess any related changes that might be taking place in other aspects of the person's functioning: his cognitions, attitudes, values, problem behaviour, etc. For example, studies have looked at self-concept (Marzillier and Winter, 1978; Percell, Berwick and Beigel, 1974), at social anxiety (Marzillier, Lambert and Kellett, 1976; Shepherd, 1977, 1978), at clinical symptoms (Trower, Yardley, Bryant and Shaw, 1978; Wilkinson, 1980), and at cognitions (Rahaim, Lefebvre and Jenkins, 1980). The behaviours and characteristics other than social behaviour which might be selected for evaluation will depend on the client population, purpose of training and theoretical interests of the trainer involved. In a school-age child, for example, it might be important to assess general classroom behaviour and academic performance if this was judged to be affected by the social skill deficit of the child.

Continuous assessment and evaluation before and after training is an important part of social skills training. It enables the trainer to monitor the progress of his clients, to develop more appropriate training programmes, and to assess his particular training methods.

This chapter has been concerned with the various ways of assessing social skill both for the purpose of identifying an individual's problems and for designing and evaluating training programmes. Assessment is fundamental to the process of social skills training and its importance cannot be overstated.

4 Basic Training Methods

There are a variety of social skills training programmes available for particular populations, problems or individuals. The basic training methods, however, will be similar whatever type of programme is chosen. The procedures used in teaching social skill resembles those used in the teaching of any other skill. The overall task is broken down into smaller stages or component parts and these are taught sysematically, step by step, starting with the simple and working toward the more complex. For each 'step' explanations and instructions are given (sometimes referred to as coaching) and this is usually followed by a demonstration (modelling). The trainee then practises the skill himself (behavioural rehearsal or role-play), feedback and encouragement (which can act as reinforcement) are given, and, if necessary, corrections are made. Finally, the newly acquired skill is practised in the home environment (homework assignments or practice).

A session would therefore typically consist of instruction, modelling, role-play, feedback and homework setting with the opportunity for clients to report on homework from the previous session. The order may vary, e.g. modelling could come before, or as part of, instruction, or a single session might cover two 'steps' and two sets of instruction and exercises, etc. would be included.

4.1   INSTRUCTION

Each session will have been designed around a particular theme (one of the 'steps') which might be a non-verbal or verbal behaviour, e.g. 'eye contact' or 'opening a conversation' or a specific social situation such as 'joining a group in the canteen at work'. The trainer drawing on his knowledge from sources, such as those given in Chapter 2, and his own and others' experience describes the behaviours to be taught in detail and explains their importance and use in social interaction, e.g. 'Looking at a person who is talking to you is an important way of showing that you are listening. It is extremely difficult to carry on talking if someone is looking away.' If the theme of a session is a particular situation, then the trainer will discuss this in terms of the appropriate behaviours involved and the social norms in that situation, e.g. 'When joining a group it is usual to look around the group as you approach, make eye contact with one of the members and make a greeting either by a nod or smile.'

It is at this stage in training that most of the cognitive aspects of social skill are covered. Instructions are given not only on the responses as such, but on the observation of the behaviours and responses of others and what they may mean in the situation. Alternative strategies and their consequences can also be explored, e.g. 'When you're talking to someone who you know usually has good eye contact and this time they're looking down at the floor, what do you think this can tell you?' 'What could you do in these circumstances?' 'What would probably be the result of doing that?' This can either take the form of question and answer as above, or be a direct talk given by the trainer. A handout, laying out the major points of the session, can be prepared in advance. This can be taken away by the client at the end of the session and used as a reminder.

It is extremely important that clear instructions are given and that they are presented using examples related to the client's own situations in a language which the client can readily understand and make sense of. Instructions are given not only to provide clients with information about social behaviour but to provide a background and rationale for the subsequent exercises and role-plays. The client should know what he is expected to do in the role-play before it takes place.

4.2 MODELLING

Modelling is a method of demonstrating appropriate behaviour. Typically, before the client takes part in the role-play, the trainer, another member of staff brought in for this purpose, or a group member (if in a group situation) gives examples of competent responses in the situation. This may involve enacting the whole role-play or just a part of it. Prepared videotapes and photographs can also be used for this purpose. It has been found that modelling is more effective when the models are of a similar age and of the same sex as the observer and when the model's behaviour is closer to that of the observer rather than highly competent or more extreme (Bandura, Grusec and Menlove, 1967).

It is important that the client does not interpret the modelled behaviour as the 'correct' way to behave, but as one of approaching a particular situation. An alternative to using modelling before the client tries it out himself (behaviour rehearsal) is to model the behaviour following the rehearsal if the client is unable to role-play the behaviour with verbal instructions alone. Modelling can also be included as part of the instructions.

Modelling has been demonstrated to be particularly useful in working with a schizophrenic population and in one study (Eisler, Blanchard, Fitts and Williams, 1978) it was found to be an essential ingredient of a training programme for improving the social skill of these clients.

4.3   BEHAVIOURAL REHEARSAL (ROLE-PLAY)

Behavioural rehearsal forms the core component of social skills training. The client, having received verbal instructions and possibly having seen the behaviour demonstrated by a role-model, enacts brief scenes which simulate real-life situations which he might encounter in his own environment. He is required to be himself in those situations, but to vary his usual set of responses and to try out new behaviours. In this way the client is enabled either to acquire new behaviours to add to his behavioural repertoire (McFall and Marston, 1970) or to increase the possibility of existing responses occurring that have been inhibited, for example by anxiety (Wolpe, 1958).

The trainer 'stage manages' the role-play, organizing any 'props' necessary for setting the scene, e.g. chairs and a desk. He might play the role of the other involved in the scene himself or, if in a group, direct a group member to play the other role or roles. This has the added benefit of providing an opportunity for members to try out completely different behaviours. Before the role-play is enacted in front of a group, members can be given the opportunity to practise for a few minutes in pairs, or threes, etc. (depending on the situation). This enables the trainer to go round giving encouragement and making suggestions before it is performed 'in public'.

When all are ready for the role-play to begin the trainer should remind the other members which specific behaviours are being trained in the session so these can be observed during the role-play and subsequent feedback be given. The role-play can now proceed.

During the role-play the client can be 'prompted' by the trainer. This can be done non-verbally, the trainer indicating through gesture to the client that he could, for example, speak a little louder, or verbal promptings can be given; 'Speak louder'. This method should only be employed when the client gets into difficulties.

If the client is unable to complete the rehearsal satisfactorily then the role-played scene should be broken down into smaller stages and rehearsed step by step. It could also be broken down into non-verbal and verbal behaviour and practised non-verbally first before adding the words.

There may be occasions when a role-play will be enacted without prior planning, such as when a client unexpectedly has a job interview the following week (Section 6.9) or in programmes which allow time for individual work (Sections 7.1 and 7.4). Here the trainer obtains information from the client about the situation and the other people involved in it, which he then uses to brief other members of the group on the roles they have to play. When the situation has occurred before, it can be useful to ask the client to behave as he did or usually does. In this way the trainer can see for himself how the person behaves and what happens rather than relying on the individual's verbal account. (If this is done it is always necessary to check with the client how accurately his behaviour represented that which occurs in the real situation.) Instruction and modelling can take place at this stage and the client can try out new behaviours. The people playing the other roles are asked to respond in role to the new behaviour.

4.4 WARM-UP EXERCISES

Canter and Wilkinson (1978) have suggested the use of warm-up exercises in addition and usually prior to, role-play. These are designed to exercise and practise, sometimes in an over-exaggerated way, the various aspects of behaviour being trained in the session but, unlike role-play, they are not generally related to actual situations. For example, a warm-up exercise on tone of voice might be to repeat a nursery rhyme happily, angrily, enthusiastically, etc. or to read a newspaper cutting in an appropriate tone of voice but slightly exaggerated. This might be followed by a role-play on talking enthusiastically about an area of interest, etc. If warm-up exercises are included it is most important that the rationale for their use is given, that the connection with the role-play is pointed out, and that they are presented in such a way that the clients perceive them as light-hearted and fun rather than silly and embarrassing.

4.5 REINFORCEMENT

After the client has obtained information about a particular skill through verbal instruction and modelling and has rehearsed the desired behaviour, his skills are shaped through reinforcement. This takes the form of feedback, whcih provides the client with information about his behaviour, and reward, which usually is praise or some appropriate incentive. The systematic use of feedback and reward shape the behaviour and increase the likelihood of it occurring again.

4.5.1 Feedback

Knowledge of results is essential to the development and improvement of a skill (Annett, 1969). Feedback can be given by the trainer, by other members of the group, or through audio or visual playback (McFall and Twentyman, 1973). If feedback is given by other group members they should be trained in advance to be positive and to present it in such a way as to be helpful to the client. The following guidelines might be useful.

(a) Behaviours for feedback should be specified in advance of the role-play so that the observers can focus on the relevant responses.

(b) Feedback should focus on the behaviour rather than on the person.

(c) Feedback should be detailed, specific and concentrate on those behaviours which have been taught either during the session or at previous sessions.

(d) Feedback on no more than three behaviours should be given at any one time since it is extremely difficult both to observe and report on a larger number.

(e) Feedback should be given directly to the individual, e.g. 'It was good the way *you* looked at her', and not 'It was good the way *she* looked at her.'

(f) Feedback should concentrate on the positive with suggestions for improvement and change if necessary, e.g. 'I thought it was good the way you came into the room and looked directly at him. I think it would have been even better if you had walked straight in without hesitating at the doorway.' Not 'It was a pity you were so hesitant at the doorway.'

(g) It should be emphasized that feedback is not an objective judgement of the individual, but a person's subjective impression which may vary from person to person.

(h) It should be remembered, particularly by the therapist, that the person giving the feedback is doing so in the light of is own norms and culture, which might differ from those of the client.

The process of giving feedback can also be of benefit. It gives the client the opportunity to practise speaking directly to another and it helps the members of a group to concentrate on the person working, keeping them involved with the group and increasing the probability of observational learning of those behaviours which are successful (and subsequently rewarded).

If video playback is used the client should, first of all, be given the opportunity to comment on his performance and the same rules of feedback should apply. Video playback, however, should be used with caution. While it can provide a source of motivation and incentive, it can also be disruptive and threatening to some individuals.

4.5.2   Rewards

Social rewards are effective reinforcers for most people (Agras, 1972) and in social skills training this is done by means of praise and encouragement. The beneficial effect of this is greatest when given immediately after the behavioural rehearsal. As well as verbal approval (praise), it can be given by facial expression, nods, applause, pats on the back, etc. Each time the client takes part in a role-play, the trainer has the opportunity to strengthen desirable behaviour with praise.

Other types of rewards can also be used but they must obviously be appropriate to the population in question, e.g. pennies for children when they have approximated the target behaviour (Twentyman and Martin, 1978), small monetary payoffs to reinforce ward social interactions of chronic psychiatric patients (Doty, 1975), stars as a reward for attendance with a mentally handicapped group (see Section 7.2).

4.6   HOMEWORK ASSIGNMENTS

Homework assignments provide an opportunity for the client to try out his newly learned behaviours in real-life conditions which are likely to produce rewarding consequences. This will enable the skills acquired in the training session to be transferred to the client's own environment (Trower, Bryant and Argyle, 1978). The importance of practising the newly learned behaviours outside sessions is stressed at the assessment stage and throughout the training. Even if the client is doing well in training sessions it is of little or no value if his behaviour in his own environment remains unchanged.

Homework assignments typically consist of behaviours corresponding to those taught in the training session which the client performs between sessions and on which he reports back in the subsequent session. For example, this might involve getting him to practise sitting in a relaxed and confident posture at least once every day, asking directions from a stranger, or joining in a conversation at work. The specific assignment will obviously depend on the type of client population and the type of situations they are likely to meet. If possible, the homework tasks should be identified by the client and the goals stated clearly. It is necessary to check carefully that the client is likely to encounter or can put himself in the situation and therefore is able to carry out his assignment. It is important that the client succeeds in his assignment, although it is advisable to warn him that, through no fault of his own, things can go wrong, e.g. he smiles at a neighbour who happens to be preoccupied, doesn't notice it and ignores him.

It can be useful for homework assignments to be written down, on a card or in a notebook. The client can then be asked to keep a record of his performance indicating what happened, when he practised the task, his success, degree of comfort or particular difficulties experienced, etc. Recording homework assignments acts to remind the client of his tasks, enables him to monitor his own behaviour and provides valuable information on which the trainer can give feedback at the subsequent session. The recording of homework with feedback can act as a powerful incentive to improvement (see example of use in Section 7.3).

Typically the client reports back at the following session on how he got on with his assignments. The trainer should obtain details of what exactly happened and the client be rewarded with appropriate praise for attempting his homework, whether he succeeded or not. If things went wrong, it is important that the trainer finds out exactly what happened and, if necessary, further training can take place.

Thinking up appropriate homework assignments for those residing in institutions may be more taxing on the imagination of the trainer and it will be necessary to obtain the co-operation of other members of staff in this, both to create opportunities for practice and to guide and reinforce behaviour. Similarly, when working with children the parents can be trained to participate in the homework assignments.

To ensure generalization of behaviour learned in sessions, it may be useful to have sessions in a variety of situations, e.g. youth clubs, the coffee bar, etc. or to create a situation where both the trainers and other group members can reinforce each other in real-life settings, e.g. out for a meal or at a disco. It would be useful for this type of practice to take place at a later stage of training when the basic skills have been acquired.

This section has provided an outline of the methods used in social skills training. The content of any programmes, i.e. what is taught (see Chapter 2) and the length, frequency and number of sessions, etc. (see Section 5.3) will depend very much on the type of client and the situation in which training takes place. The methods of training employed, however, will be similar whatever the population or setting.

5 Designing Social Skills Training Programmes

Although a number of programmes exist which have been designed for a variety of purposes and types of clients, it is preferable that trainers design their own programmes to meet the particular needs of their own clients. Detailed material from careful assessment of the clients' problems is essential in designing programmes (see Chapter 3). Information will have been obtained from the client himself, possibly also from relatives, friends or other professionals and from observation of the client at interview and, if he is in an institutionalized setting, from his day-to-day functioning. Finally, goals for training will have been set and the client will have some idea of what is expected of him. A number of decisions have then to be made before the programme can be designed. Is the client to be trained in a one-to-one or group setting? Is the programme to be designed specifically for him (individualized), or is it to be designed as a more general training course (standardized)?

5.1   GROUP OR ONE-TO-ONE TRAINING

Social skills training can be used in a one-to-one or group setting. Individual training allows concentration on the client's particular problems and may be desirable or necessary where the client is highly anxious and would find it difficult to join a group. However, group training does have a number of advantages, perhaps the most important being that the group offers a ready-made social situation which is a 'real' situation in itself. A group supplies a number of different types of people necessary for creating role-plays and for giving a greater range of feedback. The members of a group also provide a variety of models, thereby helping to dispel any idea that the therapist's modelling is the 'right' way and vicarious learning has been shown to be more effective when the models have characteristics in common with the observer (Bandura, Grusec and Menlove, 1967).

A group also provides its members with a number of people with whom they can meet and practise their newly acquired skills and can provide a supportive environment in which clients, by being with a group of people in a similar position to themselves, feel less intimidated. If there are members in the group who are further advanced in training and who report and show improvement, they can quickly help develop positive expectations in new members.

Although there are strong arguments for group training, a particular client might benefit from an initial period of one-to-one training and possibly individual sessions running concurrently with group training. In practice, the choice between one-to-one and group training frequently depends on the type of setting and the resources available. In some settings there might not be sufficient clients to form a group so one-to-one training would be necessary. In others, group training may be chosen on the basis of expediency to make more economical use of therapists' time. In both cases, however, provisions should be made to meet the needs of the individual client, i.e. the person in one-to-one training should be given the opportunity to practise in a group and those in group training the opportunity, if necessary, of one-to-one sessions.

5.2   INDIVIDUALIZED OR STANDARDIZED PROGRAMMES

Training can be designed to meet the needs of a particular individual and organized around the specific difficulties experienced. Alternatively, it can take the form of a more general social skills training course for which the client has been previously selected. For either type of training, individual or standardized, the methods employed are similar (instruction, modelling, role-play, etc.).

The individualized training programme is planned around the specific goals of the client and in each session he works on a particular aspect of his problems building up from the simple to the more complex behaviours and situations. This can be carried out in one-to-one training or in a group where each client in turn works on his own particular problem, with the other members of the group taking part in the exercises as appropriate. Such a group would be 'open' with clients joining as necessary or convenient and leaving on completion of their programmes.

The standardized programme takes the form of a set course and deals systematically with basic social skills, again building up from simple behaviours to more complex social routines. The content of any such programme would clearly depend on the type of population and purpose for which it is being designed. The needs of chronic psychiatric patients are obviously very different from those of young offenders. The programme may be designed to cover a range of social situations or confined to a specific area such as job interviews. Standardized programmes can be used in one-to-one training but are better suited to a training group. Assessment of potential clients for a standardized group is essential, but actual selection for the group might be left until after the programme has been designed.

The main advantages of standardized programmes are that once designed they can be modified and re-used, they are more easily managed than individualized programmes in group training, and trainee therapists can more readily be trained to carry out the routines. Also, a larger number of clients can be accommodated in standardized groups. However, since this type of training takes the form of a course it is necessary to run a 'closed' group which, whilst providing a safe environment for its members, is not always practicable in situations where there is a high turnover of clients, e.g. acute psychiatric admission wards. In this case an individualized programme would be more suitable. The main disadvantage of a standardized training programme is the possibility that it will not meet all the specific needs of the individuals involved.

In practice the two types of training are often combined; the first part of a programme being a general training, followed by individualized work in later sessions (Section 7.1). Material from a generalized training programme can also be adapted, if appropriate, for individualized training. As with deciding on group or one-to-one training, it is of course necessary to be sensitive to the specific requirements of each client.

5.3   DESIGNING TRAINING PROGRAMMES

While the stages and processes of designing both individualized and standardized programmes are the same, they have sufficient differences to warrant a separate discussion here. The reader is referred to the example (Figure 2) in this section of building up an individualized programme and to Section 7.1 for an example of a standardized training programme.

5.3.1   Content and plan of training

Individualized programmes

The client's goals, stated in terms of the behaviour he wishes to achieve in certain situations, plus the information about his specific deficits gained at assessment, form the basic material around which the programme is designed. The programme will consist of a number of sessions and in order to plan these sessions the material from assessment is organized to form themes. These themes may be separate behaviours, e.g. opening a conversation, facial expression, listening, or be situations which the client finds difficult, e.g. maintaining conversation at work, standing up to a teenage brother (see Chapter 2).

It is important that training both within a session and over a number of sessions progresses step by step from simple to more difficult and complex behaviours. It is necessary, therefore, to order the themes according to difficulty and in terms of a logical and meaningful progression from one stage to the next. This may necessitate a detailed breakdown of particular themes into sequences or short scenes and each scene into its behavioural components. Having conversations at work may be a theme which can then be broken down into three stages of initiating, maintaining and ending conversations, each stage to be trained separately, one building upon the other. At each stage the trainer may concentrate on the specific behavioural deficits of a client in relation to that activity, e.g. eye contact or tone of voice.

Standardized programmes

The procedure for deciding on the content and themes of a standardized programme will vary depending on the purpose of training, i.e. whether it is to be a general training in social skills (see Section 7.1) or social skills associated with a specific situation such as work (see Section 7.3), and the population for whom it is being designed. Where the clients are able to identify the situations in which they would like to develop competence, a standardized programme can be designed around those types of situations but could be more comprehensive and based not only on the deficits of particular individuals but on a wider range of situations and behaviour relevant to the population. With those clients less able to specify their training needs, the situations and themes would be identified by the trainers and others involved in the rehabilitation.

Working from the simple to the complex applies equally to the standardized programmes. Some programmes start with non-verbal behaviour and build up to verbal behaviour before progressing to quite complex situations (see Section 7.1). Others take simple situations dealing with verbal and non-verbal aspects together and gradually build up to more difficult interactions (see Section 7.2). With more specific programmes such as those for aggression management or job interviews, the order of sessions will fall into a more natural sequence in terms of the sequence of actions or events within those particular situations.

BUILDING UP AN INDIVIDUALIZED PROGRAMME

Background information

Mary West is 39, married with two teenage sons. She works in an office where she is responsible for the supervision of six girls. She has always been a shy person, finding it difficult to make friends. Three years ago she moved away from an area near her parents to a new housing estate some miles away. This coincided with her husband getting promotion at work and consequently having greater social demands made on her. Mary has found it increasingly difficult to meet people, and six months ago went to her GP complaining of depression. She showed little improvement with anti-depressant medication and was eventually referred for assessment with a view to social skills training.

Summary from assessment interview

Self-report of difficulties in social situations

Mrs West reported that she has no energy and dreads going to work where she feels taken advantage of by the juniors. She finds it difficult to allocate work to them and they tend to take the interesting jobs themselves, leaving her with the more mundane tasks. She dreads entering the boss's office, particularly if he is on the phone when she doesn't know whether to enter or come back later. She finds coffee breaks difficult and feels that she has no 'small talk'. She is terrified of going to the social functions which are a necessary part of her husband's job. She feels she has nothing to say for herself, her mind goes 'blank'. She can just about answer questions, but she does so as briefly as possible. She finds it impossible to start or continue a conversation and will avoid social contact if she can. She also finds it difficult to initiate any kind of relationships in her new neighbourhood, or to respond when a neighbour makes friendly overtures.

Figure 2.

Observations at interview

Mrs West answered questions as briefly as possible and her tone of voice was flat and monotonous. She sat slumped in the chair but would occasionally sit forward on the edge and wring her hands. Her face was, for most of the time, expressionless and her eye contact poor. She was somewhat dowdily dressed but well groomed.

Training goals (in order of difficulty)

(a) To enter the boss's office confidently
(b) To allocate work in the office, give orders and monitor progress of juniors.
(c) To be able to make friendly greetings and chat to neighbours in the street, the girls at work, etc.
(d) To be able to maintain a conversation, including initiating and responding to others both at work and at her husband's social functions.

Behavioural deficits

(a) Posture
(b) Facial expression
(c) Eye contact
(d) Vocal cues (particularly tone and volume)
(e) Giving orders
(f) Conversation openings
(g) Maintaining conversation

Outline of content of programme

This programme has been designed for six weekly sessions of about 30 minutes to be carried out in a one-to-one situation.

Session 1:	*Situation* —	Entering the boss's office, waiting a moment to see if he wishes her to enter or return later, walking across the room and sitting down.
	Behaviours —	Posture — standing, walking, sitting (confidently).
Session 2:	*Situation* —	Allocation of work, monitoring progress, giving orders.
	Behaviours —	Tone of voice (firm), eye contact, making requests (without apology).
Session 3:	*Situation* —	1. Meeting a neighbour in the street. 2. Coming into the coffee room at work.
	Behaviours —	Facial expression (friendly), tone of voice (warm), conversation openings.
Session 4:	*Situation* —	The coffee break at work.
	Behaviours —	Maintaining conversation — emphasis on listening, paying attention, making comments.
Session 5:	*Situation* —	The coffee break at work.
	Behaviours —	Maintaining conversation — emphasis on asking questions, self-disclosure, taking turns.
Session 6:	*Situation* —	Social function — joining a group, making conversation for a few minutes, moving on to another group.
	Behaviours —	Observing and assessing appropriate point of entry, joining in the conversation, ending and leaving the group.

Figure 2   [*continued*]

Detailed plan of session 1: Entering the boss's office

Welcome to the client. Recap from previous meeting on aims, length, frequency of sessions, what is expected in terms of homework and why it is important. (In subsequent sessions it is useful to start with homework feedback.)

Instruction

General introduction to non-verbal behaviour in both sending and receiving messages including why it is important in social interactions. Detailed explanation of posture — standing, walking and sitting relating it to the theme of the session, i.e. entering the boss's office confidently and sitting down. Also mention importance of interpreting non-verbal cues from boss (probably from facial expression or gesture) as signals as to whether to enter or return later.

Modelling

Trainer demonstrates the total sequence of knocking, entering, waiting, proceeding to chair and finally sitting down.

Role-play Scene: the boss's office

Part 1 Knocking on door, entering, looking at boss, waiting.
Feedback with replay, modelling and prompting as necessary.

Part 2 Walking across the room in confident manner.
Feedback with replay, modelling and prompting as necessary.

Part 3 Seated posture (confident yet relaxed).
Feedback with replay, modelling and prompting as necessary.

Part 4 The complete sequence.
Feedback with replay, modelling and prompting as necessary.

Homework assignments

1. Practise sequence each morning at work.
2. Practise relaxed and confident seated posture in different chairs twice a day.

5.3.2 Length, number and frequency of sessions

Individualized programmes

The length of each session will depend on whether the training is on an individual basis or whether the individual is part of a group, all of whose members have their own programmes, the needs of the client and the time available to the therapist. Generally speaking, it is better to cover too little than too much. However, the pace should be such that the client does not become bored or overloaded. This can be assessed during the course of training and adjustments made as necessary. In individual training anything under half an hour would probably be too short or over an hour too long. For group work the type of client is more likely to determine the length of session. For those clients who might have difficulty in concentrating, e.g. the mentally handicapped or schizophrenic person, shorter sessions of about 30-45 minutes would be advisable, whereas with out-patients or adult offenders the sessions could last up to 2 hours. The time alloted to each client within this will depend on the number in the group and whether each client is to work on his own problem in each session.

The number of sessions required will be related to the length of the sessions and the degree of difficulty of the client, varying from three to thirty or more. One advantage of group individualized training over a standard package is that one person may need only three or four sessions, whereas another may benefit from ten or twelve and both can be included in the one group.

The frequency of sessions again will vary with the type of client population and length of session. Some clients will require short but frequent sessions two or three times a week in order to reinforce newly learned behaviours and to ensure that they are not forgotten. Others will benefit from longer less-frequent sessions with sufficient time between sessions for the client to carry out his homework assignments and promote generalization to the natural setting.

Standardized programmes

As with the above, the number, length and frequency of sessions will depend upon the type of client population. In some cases the situation might determine the number of sessions, e.g. the clients might only be available for ten weeks, or a set length of time be set aside from a more general rehabilitation programme for social skills training. The length of training may vary enormously. With a fairly able population (e.g. adult offenders, out-patients) about twelve sessions is a reasonable number. With a schizophrenic population, more sessions are advisable. Very positive results have been reported from an extremely intensive training programme which included daily social skills training over a number of weeks (Wallace, 1980; Wallace, Nelson, Liberman, Aitchison, Lukoff, Elder and Ferris, 1980).

5.3.3 Designing each session

Individualized programmes

Having decided on the content or theme, order, number, length and frequency of sessions, role-play (and warm-up) exercises based on the material selected for each session can be devised and the instruction and modelling components of training worked out in detail (see Chapter 4). The exercises will be concerned with a particular individual's problem, which may be common to several individuals in a group. Role-play scenes should simulate situations or types of situation which the client might meet in his own environment, and situations with which he is experiencing difficulty (see Section 4.3). Behaviour for practice and feedback should be identified. Instruction should be pitched at a level appropriate to the population in training and should include rationale, explanation and directions (see Section 4.1). Modelling, if it is to be carried out by the therapist, should be practised prior to the session (see Section 4.2). Homework assignments should also be worked out at this stage (see Section 4.6). In designing an individualized programme to be carried out in a group, some of the exercises, particularly warm-ups, can be carried out by the whole group.

Standardized programmes

The same procedures as for individualized programmes are used except that the exercises will usually be designed around a theme selected for the session rather than an individual's problem. The theme might be some aspect of social behaviour such as eye gaze or a common social situation such as dealing with the boss at work. However, these themes should be continually related to the situations and lives of the members of the group, and role-play exercises should be designed to be appropriate both to the theme of the session and the clients for whom the programme is designed.

5.3.4   Additional exercises

The above guidelines for designing individualized and standardized programmes give the essential ingredients of the sessions to which can be added a variety of elements to help the individual and facilitate group cohesiveness, interaction and support. For example, one way of starting each session off might be for each member to say their name and something positive which they have done or has happened since the previous session (see Sections 6.8 and 7.1). This ensures that all the group members contribute to the session from the start and that the group starts on a positive note.

Warm-up exercises related to the theme of the session can also be included in the programme although these are probably more successful when used in group rather than one-to-one training (see Sections 4.4 and 7.1).

Games which may or may not be related to the content of the session can be included, if appropriate, but this will largely depend on the population for whom the programme is being designed (Pfeiffer and Jones, 1979). Games are one way of 'teaching' people to have fun and let go. Also, people will behave within the context of a game in a way that they would find difficult if presented with an exercise, e.g. raising the volume of their voice. It is advisable for the therapist to be clear why he is including these and to present the rationale to his clients (see Section 7.2).

Some therapists have found the inclusion of anxiety management procedures useful when working with anxious clients (Goldfried, 1977). This can be carried out on an individual basis, or form part of group training.

5.4   GROUP COMPOSITION

With individualized training in which each member spends some time working on his particular difficulty, the group needs to be quite small, between four and six members, to ensure that everybody has some time to work. With standardized programmes numbers can vary according to population and the number of therapists available. Less than six makes rather a small group and over fourteen probably too large. The type of client who needs more attention would probably benefit from a smaller group.

There is some discussion amongst trainers as to whether clients in a general social skills training group should be of similar age, intelligence, diagnosis, social group and with similar types of difficulties, or whether it is better to mix different types of clients in one group. There are no rules for this. Clients with some characteristics in common might feel that other group members have a better understanding of their difficulties and can be more supportive. However, some mix provides a variety of models, personnel for role-play and a greater range of feedback. In addition, the client can gain a better understanding of people from a wider sphere.

The question invariably arises for those working in a psychiatric setting as to the advisability of mixing people with different clinical diagnoses in one group. As the problems dealt with in a group are the social skills problems (and for some clients the presenting of psychiatric symptoms would be secondary to these) clients from different diagnostic categories can generally be included in a single group. However, because of the particular difficulties encountered by the schizophrenic client, it might be desirable to keep the proportion of schizophrenic to non-psychotic members to a minimum. Here the therapist must use his judgement as to the advisability of the mix. This would apply to both individualized and standardized training.

5.5   SOCIAL SKILLS TRAINING WITHIN THE BROADER THERAPEUTIC OR TRAINING CONTEXT

Social skills training may be the only type of treatment or training necessary for a particular individual's problem. However, it is frequently used in conjunction with other therapies or as part of a more comprehensive training programme.

Where lack of social skills is only one of the client's difficulties he may be receiving therapy for other aspects of his problem concurrently with social skills training. If the same therapist is involved then there should be little difficulty in combining various therapeutic approaches, although both the client and the therapist should be clear about which approach is being used to tackle which problems. If the client is receiving other treatment from a different therapist, care must be taken to clarify the objectives of the various methods for the client so that he avoids becoming confused. This requires careful preparation of the client as well as good co-operation and communication between therapists (see Sections 6.1 and 6.2).

Social skills training often forms part of a broader training programme, e.g. in rehabilitation programmes for long-term prisoners or chronic psychiatric patients, in sex education for the mentally handicapped person, and in the teaching of living and job skills to adolescents. In such cases the design of the social skills programme should not be carried out in isolation from other aspects of the programme but should be an integral part of an overall plan tailored to fit in at the appropriate time with the teaching of other skills. It is of little value, for example teaching the social skill aspect of shopping, job finding and socializing to institutionalized clients in isolation from the practical living skills such as knowing where shops are, what food to buy, how to get to shops, to find jobs, to complete application forms, etc. The two are interwoven and it is necessary to design a programme to integrate the skills. Team effort is therefore essential so that all members involved with clients are clear about their aims and differential responsibilities.

This chapter has demonstrated how the material from assessment is used to plan and design programmes for both individuals and groups. The success of social skills training is dependent on having a well-designed programme that not only meets the needs of particular individuals, but which is practical and sensible in terms of the time and resources available.

6 Preparation for and Management of Social Skills Training

Having carried out a detailed assessment of the client's difficulties and designed an appropriate social skills training programme, all that remains is to carry out the training! Careful assessment and good planning minimize the problems of managing the training. However, as with any other form of training or therapy, successful social skills training presupposes a high level of competence and therapeutic skills on the part of the trainer. No manual can give this, but this chapter looks at some of the more important features concerned with the preparation and management of training. Some of these points will have been made elsewhere but are repeated here to emphasize their importance.

6.1   PREPARING THE CLIENT

The client will have been seen for an assessment of his specific problems (Chapter 3). Before embarking on a social skills programme it is important that the client is well prepared and a further meeting may be necessary to ensure that he has some understanding of the purpose of the training, the form it will take and what is expected of him. The level and detail of the explanation will of course depend upon the particular client and context in which the programme is to take place.

It is important too that the client understands that the purpose of the programme is to enable him to achieve the goals that have been set. He can be given an explanation of the social skills approach and an outline of the methods to be used so that he will be clear about what he can expect.

Details of the arrangements for sessions should be given and punctuality, regular attendance, commitment and full co-operation of the client should be stressed. A number of procedures can be used to enhance the motivation and co-operation of clients. Training can be made conditional upon regular attendance, with the client required to account satisfactorily for absences. This is particularly important when working with clients in the community. With children, chronic psychiatric patients or mentally handicapped persons, it may be useful to have an inbuilt incentive scheme such as a token system of rewards for attending sessions (see Sections 4.5.2 and 7.2). To ensure commitment to a programme a contract system can be used which lays out the aims of the programme plus what the therapist agrees to supply and the client to attempt (Kanfer and Karoly, 1972). Contracts can be powerful motivation for those who need an external nudge. They are particularly useful for homework assignments providing a necessary incentive since both reward from the therapist and other participants and continuation in the programme is dependent on achievements, plus attempts to achieve, outside the training situation.

The importance of homework should be explained and emphasized so that the client understands that practising the skills outside the training session is as equally important as participating in the session itself. He may be required to keep a homework assignment book in which to record his homework tasks, performance and achievements, and this should be explained to him. It can provide a useful incentive in some cases (see Sections 4.6 and 7.3).

If a client is to attend a group he should be told who the group members are likely to be and the value of the group in giving support and encouragement as well as offering the opportunity to meet with others in a similar position. He should also be told that everyone in the group is expected to participate, including the therapist, and the object is to have fun as well as to learn from it.

6.2 THE TRAINERS

The trainer should have skills to establish a warm and trusting relationship with his client and this can be built up at the assessment stage.

This will facilitate the client's understanding of his difficulties and help him accept the training. Having a good relationship with the client will enable him to work in the sessions and enhance the trainer's effectiveness as a 'reinforcer'. If the trainer is to run a group, experience in group skills is beneficial. These can be acquired by participating in a training group and by assisting an experienced trainer. Potential trainers often ask whether it is necessary to be highly socially skilled to conduct training groups. The trainer should be reasonably competent but more important is an understanding of social interaction and strategies for overcoming difficulties in social situations.

With one-to-one sessions it is usual to have only one trainer. However, it may be useful and possible to enlist the help of staff members for work on specific areas where it is important to have extra people for a role-play or where a female trainer requires a male person to role-play for a client with particular difficulties with male figures. If this is the case it should be planned and arranged in advance and the staff member should be fully briefed as to what is required of him.

In group training it is advisable to have at least two trainers working with the group. A male and female trainer will obviously offer the best combination of models, but if this is not possible same sex trainers can work effectively together. Two trainers are advisable for both managing the exercises and coping with the extensive demands placed on them in organizing and running such a group. If video is to be used, one trainer is needed to operate the equipment and a second to organize the role-play and feedback.

It is essential, if there are to be two trainers, that they work out complementary roles from the outset. Both should be involved in the assessment of clients if possible. This is particularly important for those working together for the first time.

Careful and detailed planning is essential for a successful social skills programme. In both a one-to-one and a group individualized programme, there will be more flexibility within sessions, but none the less, an overall plan and design of exercises is desirable. Where there are two trainers involved this should be done together throughout and decisions about type and content of programme for particular clients' problems jointly made.

It is extremely important that both trainers know clearly in advance who is doing what in the session. Because social skills training is highly demanding of the trainer and needs careful directing, it is useful to split up a session with trainers taking it in turns to instruct and set up and run exercises. Each trainer should have his job to do and be able to give support to the other when necessary. From the outset frank discussion between the trainers should take place and a feedback session after each session is useful. Those sessions will allow the trainers to iron out problems in planning as well as meshing of their training skills. Problems between trainers, if unresolved, greatly disrupt the smooth and effective running of a group.

Finally, as discussed in previous sections, it is important that trainers establish good working relationships with their referring agents and with other trainers or therapists that may be involved with their clients in other capacities. Regular feedback between those involved with a client will enhance colleagues' understanding of the social skills approach which will facilitate appropriate referral and avoid confusion and misunderstanding.

6.3 VISITORS AND TRAINEE THERAPISTS

It is useful for trainers to decide at the outset their policy on admitting visitors or trainee trainers to the sessions. It is not advisable to have visitors as observers and a useful rule is that they participate in the exercises. Trainee trainers, similarly, should be expected to participate in the sessions and their role, whether as client participators or trainers, made explicit both to themselves and to the clients.

With a closed group, as in a standardized programme, it is advisable to insist that visitors attend all sessions as group members because occasional attendance can be disruptive to the support and cohesiveness of the group. This may be less likely to occur in an open group with an individualised training programme because the group will be more used to people coming and going. It is advisable however to plan the visits in advance and to let the clients know what to expect.

6.4 SIGNIFICANT OTHERS

The object of social skills training is to change the interpersonal behaviour of the client. This will inevitably mean that if effective it will change his behaviour in relation to those with whom he is in contact. It may be necessary, depending on the client, to discuss with those persons most likely to be affected by the change what they can expect and to enlist their co-operation. For example, when working with children it would be necessary to involve the family so that parents can understand what and how the child is attempting to learn and be able to participate, for instance in the homework tasks. Similarly, it will be important to discuss with a wife or husband the changes that may take place in his or her spouse. This may be particularly important if the client is in an institution where contact with the family members is not a frequent occurrence, e.g. prison.

If working within an institutional setting, the client will be returning to his ward or domestic setting and his attendants or nurses should be involved in his training at the outset. They should be included in a discussion of the aims of the training and their assistance sought at the assessment stage where they can provide valuable observational information. They play a vital role in guiding and reinforcing the new behaviour of the clients acquired in the training sessions and can give valuable feedback to the trainers on the progress the client is making. There is little point in shaping up a person's conversational skills in training if when they return to the ward they are told to 'shut up' as the staff haven't got time to talk to them!

6.5   THE ENVIRONMENT

In one-to-one training it is most likely that an office environment will be used. If this is the case it should provide enough space and be furnished in a flexible manner to provide the opportunity for setting up role-plays. With groups a large room that will accommodate the group comfortably with space to move around in is necessary. Easy chairs and a carpeted floor are desirable. A blackboard or large sheets of paper which can be pinned to walls are also useful. There should be sufficient materials and furniture to be used as props in the role-plays, such as glasses in pub scenes, a telephone, or substitute props, e.g. a coat stand for a bus stop. Privacy is an important factor and sessions should run uninterrupted and unobserved.

In some instances it may be necessary to follow the training sessions with in situ training, e.g. taking chronic patients into a pub so that their performance can be monitored and guided. In such cases the place should be carefully checked out by the trainer beforehand so that any possible difficulties can be dealt with.

6.6   PARTICIPATION AND INVOLVEMENT IN TRAINING

In a one-to-one situation the trainer can directly encourage and involve the client in training with discussion, reinforcement and feedback. With group training extra effort may have to be made to encourage all members of the group to participate fully and thereby become involved with their own and others' training and progress.

Participation can be achieved by questions and discussion following instruction and by using group members to model behaviours which they can demonstrate effectively. Everyone should take his turn in the role-play exercises, with group members playing the parts of others in the role-play. The rest of the group should then be involved in giving feedback. This can be done verbally, following the guidelines suggested in Section 4.5.1, or members can allocate marks for the specific behaviours using, for example, three fingers for excellent, could not be improved; two for very good, but needs some work; one for all right, but needs quite a lot of work. Clients can then be asked to explain why they have given a particular rating. This ensures that the rest of the group pays attention to the client working and also helps them to develop observational skills that might be useful outside training. In order for them to do this effectively of course they must be able to see clearly what takes place in the role-play and this may necessitate organizing them into appropriate positions in the room.

If a client opts out of role-play, the therapist must find out why. Is it because he thought it stupid? (It might be!) Is it because he found it too difficult? If so, the role-played scene can be broken down and tackled step by step by the client, with modelling as necessary (see Chapter 4). The client should be encouraged, but if he is pushed into doing something which is too difficult he is less likely to co-operate in further training. Similarly, if the client did not attempt the homework, why not? Was it because it was too difficult? If so further training may be necessary or the task broken down into smaller steps. Encouragement and suggestions from other members may also help him. Did the client understand what was expected of him? Further explanation might be necessary. Did he forget? Record cards or notebooks can be essential. Homework assignment books and homework reporting also facilitate involvement because each group member is required to say how he got on and can be given feedback and encouragement from the other members. Was it that he couldn't be bothered? In this case a contract, making therapy dependent upon completion of homework, may be necessary. Alternatively, an incentive scheme related to homework completion could be used, e.g. points awarded for each assignment, graphically displayed to indicate progress (see Section 7.3).

Other methods not directly related to the actual training can be included to encourage participation, such as opening introductions, positive event reporting (see Sections 5.3.4 and 7.1), games (see Sections 5.3.4 and 7.2) and farewells at the end of a session. The therapist should be clear about the rationale of the inclusion of such exercises and, as with the training, they must be carefully thought out and appropriate to the population for whom they are designed.

6.7   MAINTAINING A BEHAVIOURAL APPROACH

In social skills training it is essentially behaviour which is being taught. People will, of course, come with their own feelings, attitudes, opinions and perceptions of themselves and others which are likely to emerge and probably change during the course of training.

However, it is extremely important that a behavioural approach is maintained and that the client, who will have been prepared for this at the assessment stage, is encouraged to concentrate on acquiring and practising new behaviour during session time. This is not to say that thoughts and feelings are not important and should be ignored, only that they should, if appropriate, be explored within the context of the behaviour being taught. A more general discussion with the client of his problems or any difficulties he may be experiencing with the training model should take place at a separate session. When working with individual clients the trainer may include social skills training within a more general discussion of problems. However, it is important that the trainer structures his session so that he is able to concentrate on the behaviour of the client when working with his social skill difficulties.

Training is, of course, always concerned with specific aspects of behaviour and even in dealing with role-plays of quite complex interactions it is necessary to identify in advance the key behaviours on which to concentrate (see Chapter 3). Giving feedback should also encourage clients to think in terms of specific behaviours rather than making value judgements about a client's performance (see Section 4.5.1).

Questions to the client about his performance in homework tasks or role-plays should always be phrased in behavioural terms. The trainer should avoid asking the client questions such as 'how did you feel?', but ask 'what was good about the way you did it?' followed by 'how could you have improved on it?', thereby encouraging the client to think about his performance in terms of his behaviour in the situation. Similarly, when the client comments on his feelings about his performance rather than his behaviour, he should be encouraged to formulate what was good or not so good about his behaviour.

Frequently, at the start of training, a client may say that it 'doesn't feel like me' when suggestions for behavioural change are made, for example to increase voice volume. The client should nevertheless be encouraged to try out the new behaviour and practise it for a period of time to give the opportunity for the behaviour to become integrated into his behavioural repertoire. If he still maintains that it is not right after a period of time, then the instructions should be modified.

By maintaining a behavioural approach and making it clear that, for the moment, it is just behaviour which is being practised, an environment is created in which the client can try out a range of behaviours free from the value judgement of others and from the limitations of his own self-perceptions.

6.8   MAINTAINING A POSITIVE APPROACH

The atmosphere of a social skills training session should always be positive and supportive, with the emphasis on what the client can and is working to achieve rather than on his deficits and failures. Role-play exercises and homework assignments should be pitched at a level which enable the client to succeed, and social reinforcement in the form of abundant and enthusiastic praise should be given for any achievement, however small. If the client has been unsuccessful in carrying out any operation, then he can be rewarded for trying, and, if necessary, the exercise or assignment can be broken down into small stages and tried again.

Feedback should always concentrate on the positive aspects, with suggestions for improvement (see Section 4.5.1) and the therapist should be persistant in interrupting any negative feedback by asking the group member to re-phrase it in positive terms.

Methods can be devised for starting the session on a positive note, e.g. positive event reporting. The therapist might have to probe a little with some clients to elicit something positive, but he should not give up.

Finally, maintaining a positive approach does not mean that the therapist ignores or is oblivious to a person or persons in the group who may be agitated or distressed. An experienced therapist will be able to be sensitive to this and keep the group positive at the same time.

6.9 MAINTAINING A STRUCTURED BUT FLEXIBLE PROGRAMME

Although emphasis has been placed in this manual on the planning and preparation of sessions in advance, in any real situation the unexpected is bound to occur. A client might suddenly get an interview for a job, be asked out for a date or have to face a new boss. When this type of situation, which is obviously important to the client, arises, time can be set aside for training on the new situation, involving other members as much as possible. For example, they could be consulted as to how much time is to be spent on the role-play and discuss the possible ways of handling the situation.

Sometimes it happens that, as training proceeds, the client turns out to have social skill difficulties other than those identified at assessment. A reassessment can then be made and any necessary adjustments made to the programme.

6.10 IN CONCLUSION

As must be apparent in this manual, social skills training is a specific, directive and highly structured form of training requiring careful identification of problems and detailed preparation of programmes, therapists and clients. It is organized but not rigid and will no doubt continue to develop and change. Whilst most trainers and clients find it a demanding form of training, they usually also find it highly rewarding, stimulating and fun.

7 Social Skills Training Programmes

These programmes have been designed, or are based on those designed by practitioners in different fields for their own clients. They are included here as examples of the various types of programmes currently being used. They are written as notes for the trainer and it is hoped that the reader will find them helpful in designing programmes for his own population rather than as blueprints for training. Further information on any of the programmes can be obtained directly from the practitioners themselves.

7.1 SOCIAL SKILLS TRAINING PROGRAMME FOR A PSYCHIATRIC OUT-PATIENT POPULATION
Devised by Sandra Canter and Jill Wilkinson, University of Surrey, Guildford.

This programme was designed and is used as a general standardized training in social skill. The clients for the groups are men and women of various ages and clinical diagnoses, some of whom would be involved in other forms of therapy or be seen for additional individualized social skills sessions.

The programme consists of twelve weekly 2-hour sessions with two therapists and a maximum of fourteen participants.

SESSION 1

NON-VERBAL BEHAVIOUR I: POSTURE, GAIT, PERSONAL DISTANCE, GESTURE

1. *WELCOME* to the group.

2. *INTRODUCTION TO THERAPISTS*. We introduce ourselves by our first names and say a little about ourselves.

3. *ROUND-THE-GROUP NAMES*. Each person gives his first name in turn and we go round the group about three times, slowly.

4. *INTRODUCTION TO SOCIAL SKILLS TRAINING,* including what it is, some of the techniques used during training, and what is expected of members in terms of participation, commitment and homework tasks.

5. *INSTRUCTION*
   General talk on non-verbal behaviour, its importance and function (see Section 2.1). Emphasis on gait, posture, distance and gesture discussed within a range of situational contexts (see Sections 2.1.3, 2.1.4 and 2.1.5).

6. *WARM-UP EXERCISE* (Posture)
   (Before introducing this exercise the rationale for warm-ups is explained, see Section 4.4).

   Therapists choose pairs who sit in chairs opposite each other. Everyone is asked to 'freeze', i.e. keep absolutely still and to become aware of, and remember, both his own posture and that of his partner. Then one partner of each pair can 'unfreeze' and he then is instructed to prompt (using verbal, gestural and physical prompts) his partner into a relaxed, confident posture. He then checks this out with his partner and together they adjust the posture if necessary. The aim of this exercise is to achieve a posture which both looks to others and feels to the person himself, relaxed and confident. The couples then reverse roles and the other partner adopts the posture he initially froze and is prompted into his relaxed and confident posture. Again, this is checked out and adjusted if necessary. During this sequence the therapists go round the pairs giving feedback and helping out where necessary.

7. *WARM-UP EXERCISE* (Gait)
Group and therapists mill around the room
(a) with exaggerated soggy gait,
(b) strutting and cocky,
(c) relaxed and confident.

8. *WARM-UP EXERCISE* (Distance)
In pairs. One partner stands still, the other advances and stops at a comfortable distance. He then checks out with his partner whether the distance is too near, too far, just right and makes adjustments as necessary. Reverse roles and repeat.

9. *WARM-UP EXERCISE* (Gesture)
In pairs. Each partner in turn describes the house he lives in using
(a) grand exaggerated gestures,
(b) appropriate gestures.

10. *ROLE-PLAY*
(Before role-play is set up, therapists give instructions on observation and giving feedback; see Section 4.5.1.)
Situation. Entering a pub and joining a friend. One partner enters, sees friend by bar, gestures, walks across, stops at appropriate distance, gestures to a table and sits down.
Behaviours for feedback. Gait, gesture, posture.
Procedure. Practised in pairs, each person taking a turn and presented to the group for feedback.

11. *HOMEWORK*
Twice a day practise sitting and walking in a relaxed and confident manner.

12. *GAME* (see Section 5.3.4).

SESSION 2

NON-VERBAL BEHAVIOUR II: FACIAL EXPRESSION, EYE CONTACT, TONE OF VOICE

1. *NAME AND POSITIVE EVENT REPORT* (see Section 5.3.4)
   (Each person introduces himself and reports something good which has happened during the previous week.)

2. *HOMEWORK FEEDBACK* (see Chapters 4 and 6 and Section 6.6)

3. *INSTRUCTION*
   Talk on eye contact, facial expression and tone of voice with emphasis on their importance in expressing emotion (see Sections 2.1.1, 2.1.2 and 2.1.8).

4. *WARM-UP EXERCISE* (Eye contact)
   Group mills around room, looking around. When therapist says stop, clients pair up and maintain eye contact for 3 seconds. Repeat several times.

5. *WARM-UP EXERCISE* (Facial expression)
   List of emotional states on board (e.g. happy, sad, angry, contemptuous, bored, enthusiastic, interested). Therapist whispers to each client in turn which emotion he has to portray through facial expression. Group guesses. Therapist models and prompts as necessary.

6. *WARM-UP EXERCISE* (Emotional tone)
   In pairs sitting back-to-back on floor one partner recites a nursery rhyme in an emotional tone chosen from list (as in previous exercise). Other partner has to guess. Reverse roles and repeat.

7. *ROLE-PLAY*

Situation. Greeting (hello, hi, etc.) someone as you pass them in the street
(a) in a warm, friendly manner,
(b) formally.
Behaviours for feedback. Facial expression, eye contact, tone of voice.
Procedure. Practise both modes in pairs and present one to group for feedback and rating.

8. *HOMEWORK*

Get each person to identify a situation in which to practise a non-verbal greeting. Practise every day.

9. *GAME*

SESSION 3

NON-VERBAL BEHAVIOUR III: VOCAL CUES

1. *NAME AND POSITIVE EVENT REPORT*

2. *HOMEWORK FEEDBACK*

3. *INSTRUCTION*
   Talk on vocal cues, i.e. tone, volume, pitch, redundancies, fluency. Emphasis on their importance in expressing emotion, showing feeling and gauging the other's mood (see Section 2.1.8).

4. *WARM-UP EXERCISE* (Volume)
   In pairs. Sitting opposite each other one partner recites a nursery rhyme as loudly then as quietly as possible. Partner encourages by gesture, facial expression, etc. Reverse and repeat.

5. *WARM-UP EXERCISE* (Speed)
   As above, but this time as quickly as possible then slowly and drawn out.

6. *WARM-UP EXERCISE* (Pitch)
   As above, but this time starting the rhyme at the bottom end of the scale and working up to a high pitch and down again.

7. *WARM-UP EXERCISE* (Tone)
   In two small groups.
   (a) Each person reads a 'neutral' newspaper article in a specified tone of voice.
   (b) Next time round each person reads a more emotionally charged article in a tone appropriate to the content, but slightly exaggerated.

8. *ROLE-PLAY*

Situation. In pub (as in Session 1) client enters, sees 'long-lost' acquaintance, walks over, says something like, 'Hello, I haven't seen you for a long time.' Acquaintance asks if he would like a drink, gets it, client suggests they should sit down and says enthusiastically: 'What have you been doing since I last saw you?' Acquaintance says: 'Well, it's been a bit hard, I've been out of work for the last 6 months.' Client replies with appropriate tone, 'Oh, I'm sorry to hear that.'

Behaviours for feedback. Tone of voice, volume, pitch.

Procedure. Practised in pairs and presented to the group for feedback and rating.

9. *HOMEWORK*

(a) Every day greet someone using friendly tone of voice (remembering facial expression, etc.).

(b) Each day note down what someone's tone of voice told you about their mood (were they friendly, bored, angry).

10. *GAME*

SESSION 4

VERBAL BEHAVIOUR I: LISTENING, ENCOURAGING THE OTHER TO TALK, ASKING QUESTIONS

1. *NAME AND POSITIVE EVENT REPORT*

2. *HOMEWORK FEEDBACK*

3. *INSTRUCTION*
   Talk on conversation with emphasis on listening (stressing the role of non-verbal behaviour, particularly eye contact, facial expression and posture), and drawing the other person out by use of questions, picking up cues and reflecting back (see Section 2.2.2.1).

4. *WARM-UP EXERCISE* (Listening)
   In two groups, one therapist per group. Each member of small group takes it in turn to listen and show he is listening while the therapist, or another client, talks about a topic of general interest (e.g. where he went on holiday).

5. *WARM-UP EXERCISE* (Encouraging the other to talk)
   As before, but this time client has to ask questions, respond to cues and reflect back.

6. *ROLE-PLAY EXERCISE*
   Situation. At work. A new person has started work that day and the client has to draw him out by asking questions, reflecting back and listening.
   Behaviours for feedback. Questions — appropriateness and number, eye contact.
   Procedure. Practised in pairs and presented to the group for feedback and rating.

7. *HOMEWORK*

Ask clients individually to identify situations in which they can practise listening and encouraging the other to talk. They are instructed to do this once a day.

8. *GAME*

SESSION 5

VERBAL BEHAVIOUR II: TALKING, MAINTAINING CONVERSATION

1. *NAME AND POSITIVE EVENT REPORT*

2. *HOMEWORK FEEDBACK*

3. *INSTRUCTION I* (Talking)
   Choosing a topic appropriate to person and situation, current interests, etc. Levels of disclosure from fact to feeling (see Section 2.2.2.1).

4. *WARM-UP EXERCISE* (Description)
   In two groups, one therapist per group. Each person takes 1 minute to describe some activity in which he has engaged in the last week (e.g. preparing a meal, going to a football match).

5. *WARM-UP EXERCISE* (Self-disclosure)
   In same groups. Each person takes 1½ minutes to talk about himself with the rest of the group giving attention. He starts off with 'I'm ... and I ...', but not repeating what he has said about himself until his time is up.

6. *INSTRUCTION II* (Maintaining conversation)
   Emphasizing the use of non-verbal behaviour in hand-over of conversation (see Section 2.2.2.2). Therapists can model this.

7. *WARM-UP EXERCISE* (Conversation)
   In pairs.
   (a) Therapist gives specific topic for a 2-minute conversation. This is repeated with another topic.
   (b) Trainer gives two topics and clients have to change from one topic to the other.

Suggested topics: the weather, holidays, public versus private transport, current affairs, music.

8. *ROLE-PLAY*

   Situation. At a bus stop. Client is joined by someone he knows but hasn't seen for some time, who starts conversation by saying, 'I haven't seen you for a long time'. They continue for about 3 minutes.

   Behaviours for feedback. Appropriateness of content, picking up cues, handing over.

   Procedure. Practised in pairs then presented to group for feedback. Each pair has just one conversation and half the group observe and gives feedback on one partner, the other half on the other.

9. *HOMEWORK*

   One conversation each day with someone you know.

10. *GAME*

SESSION 6

VERBAL BEHAVIOUR III: OPENING AND CLOSING CONVERSATIONS

1. *NAME AND POSITIVE EVENT REPORT*

2. *HOMEWORK FEEDBACK*

3. *INSTRUCTION I* (Introductions)
   Of self to another and of two people to each other.

4. *WARM-UP EXERCISE* (Introductions)
   In a circle. One person starts, introduces person on left to person on right, gives names and some small piece of information about each or something they have in common, e.g. 'John, this is Harry, I think you both went to the same school.' Proceed round the circle.

5. *INSTRUCTION II* (Initiating conversation)
   This could take the form of a discussion. Elicit from group possible ways of initiating conversation (see Section 2.2.2.2).

6. *WARM-UP EXERCISE* (Initiating conversation)
   Group mills around the room. Each person has to stop and make opening remark to at least four people.

7. *INSTRUCTION III* (Ending a conversation)
   This again could take the form of a discussion (see Section 2.2.2.2).

8. *ROLE-PLAY*

Situation. In pub. Client is seated with friend, third person approaches who is known only to client, who introduces him to friend, initiates and maintains conversation then leaves.

Behaviours for feedback. Introduction, opening sequence, parting sequence.

Procedure. Introduction, opening remark and closing practised in threes, then whole sequence presented to the group for feedback and rating.

9. *HOMEWORK*

Open, maintain and close a conversation at least once a day.

10. *GAME*

SESSION 7

ASSERTIVE BEHAVIOUR I: STANDING UP FOR YOURSELF

1. *NAME AND POSITIVE EVENT REPORT*

2. *HOMEWORK FEEDBACK*

3. *INSTRUCTION*
   General talk on what is meant by assertion in this context (see Section 2.3) emphasizing standing up for yourself without being aggressive or argumentative. Important behaviours would include firm tone of voice, steady eye gaze, straight posture, being polite without being apologetic. Types of situations might include taking a faulty article back to a shop, disagreeing or arguing a point, dealing with high-pressure sales people, coping with criticism or being provoked, speaking out in a group, dealing with someone who takes unilateral decisions which affect you (e.g. changing the TV channel), asking for a rise or better conditions at work, giving instructions or orders.

4. *ROLE-PLAY*
   Situation. Each person identifies a specific situation or type of situation in which he has difficulty being assertive (he might be overly timid or aggressive).
   Behaviours for feedback. Relevant to the individual situation but tone of voice and posture usually important.
   Procedure. Each person in turn describes a situation and client and therapists set up a role-play of what actually happened. Suggestions are made for different behaviours and alternative strategies, the scene repeated and feedback given.

5. *HOMEWORK*
   Practise role-played situation if possible. If not practicable then choose another situation requiring assertive behaviour, e.g. buying an article the wrong size and taking it back to change it.

SESSION 8

ASSERTIVE BEHAVIOUR II: ASKING, ACCEPTING, TURNING DOWN

1. *NAME AND POSITIVE EVENT REPORT*

2. *HOMEWORK FEEDBACK*

3. *INSTRUCTION*
   Asking. Emphasis on being direct, looking at the other (unless on the telephone), making it clear what you want (whether it is to ask someone out or a favour).
   Checking-out procedures. Discuss ways of checking-out whether he/she is interested before actually asking him/her out. This minimizes chance of refusal or embarrassment. Model (see Section 2.3.2).
   Recovery from refusal. When you ask someone out and they turn you down, it is important to acknowledge your feelings about being turned down but ending with a positive statement leaving your options open, e.g. 'I'm sorry you can't/don't want to come. I'll call you again some time' (see Section 2.3.3).
   Accepting. Emphasize being positive about accepting by tone of voice. Whether it's 'Yea O.K.' or 'Yes I would like to go', the message can be the same.
   Turning down. Important to get the message you intend across. If you are saying 'no' to an unreasonable request then it is important to say 'no' and not make unnecessary excuses. If you don't want to go out with someone then maybe one excuse might act as a 'face-saver' for the other person but no more. If you would like to help or go out with this person but can't for some reason then make this clear, e.g. 'I would have liked to come but unfortunately I've already made arrangements for Monday evening' followed by an alternative 'I could go on Tuesday' or 'maybe next time' (see Section 2.3.4).

4. *WARM-UP EXERCISE* (Saying 'no')
   In circle (or group can be split into two). One person starts by making an unreasonable request to the person on his left, e.g. 'I know you're not doing anything this weekend, I wonder if you could drive me to

Lands End to see my sister who has just had triplets'. The other has to respond first by recognizing the asker's need, 'I know how much you want to see your sister' followed by a firm, 'but no,' with no excuses. He then turns to the person on his left with a request, etc.

5. *WARM-UP EXERCISE* (Asking, accepting, turning down and recovery) In a circle as before. This time the first person asks the person on his left to do something (reasonable) or to go out with him. His request is accepted enthusiastically. This person then turns to his left with a request or invitation which is turned down because the person doesn't want to comply. The person asking then has to make a recovery statement. The next time the person turns the invitation down because he can't accept, the next accepts and so on.

6. *ROLE-PLAY*
   Situation. Individuals can choose whether to carry this out on a telephone or face to face. They set the scene themselves. In pairs, one person asks the other out. He responds by
   (a) accepting,
   (b) turning down because he doesn't want to go, and
   (c) turning down because he can't go.
   If the asker is accepted then arrangements are made to meet; if turned down because the other can't make it then alternative arrangements made; if turned down flat then he makes a recovery.
   Behaviours for feedback
   (a) For asker: making it clear what he wanted, tone of voice, follow up arrangements/recovery.
   (b) For respondent: making message clear, tone of voice.
   Procedure. Practised in pairs and presented to the group for feedback. Half the group observe and give feedback on one partner, the other half on the other partner. Reverse roles and repeat.

7. *HOMEWORK*
   Group members make arrangements to telephone each other with a request or invitation. This must be 'real', e.g. 'Could you meet me for coffee, ten minutes before the group meet next week?' The respondent can then accept or turn down the invitation. Additionally, if anyone has an actual situation which they would like to practise this can be done as part of their homework.

SESSION 9

ASSERTIVE BEHAVIOUR III: PAYING AND RECEIVING COMPLIMENTS, SHOWING AFFECTION

1. *NAME AND POSITIVE EVENT REPORT*

2. *HOMEWORK FEEDBACK*

3. *INSTRUCTION I*
   Paying a compliment is a way of showing you like someone. Comments can be about appearance, 'I like that jacket you're wearing', about something the person has done, 'You've made a really good job of that', or about the person themself, 'You always strike me as a very understanding person (see Section 2.3.5).
   Receiving a compliment. Accept it with thanks or by positive non-verbal signals, don't deny it, shrug it off or invalidate it.

4. *WARM-UP EXERCISE* (Paying and receiving compliments)
   One person stands on a chair in the centre of the room. Others mill about and each has to pay a compliment to the person in the middle who has to receive it appropriately. Repeat until everyone has had a turn in the middle.

5. *INSTRUCTION II* (Showing affection)
   Emphasize getting the level right, and checking out by being sensitive to feedback from the other. Affection shown by physical proximity, touch, tone of voice, facial expression, terms of endearment, paying compliments, listening, taking an interest, responding positively and remembering things which are important to the other, likes and dislikes.

6. *WARM-UP EXERCISE* (Showing affection)
   Group forms two lines at opposite ends of room. One person from each line walks or runs towards the other and they meet in the centre

of the room, greet each other enthusiastically, as if meeting a long-lost friend at a station. Repeat until all members have had a turn.

7. *ROLE-PLAY*

Situation. After an evening out with a friend, boyfriend, girlfriend, husband, wife or lover. In the car or walking home (each individual chooses the situation). Affectionate interchange about how much they enjoyed the evening, each other's company, etc.

Behaviours for feedback. Proximity/touch, positive content, tone of voice.

Procedure. Practised in pairs and presented to the group for feedback. Half the group give feedback on one partner, the other half on the other partner.

8. *HOMEWORK*

Pay a compliment or have a positive interaction at least three times during the week.

SESSIONS 10 AND 11

INDIVIDUAL WORK

1. *NAME AND POSITIVE EVENT REPORT*

2. *HOMEWORK FEEDBACK*

3. *ROLE-PLAYS*
   Individuals identify any remaining areas of difficulty and three or four per session are role-played, first as it happened, then instructions and suggestions can be made by therapists and group and scene role-played again (see Section 4.3). Some of the scenes listed below might be useful to work on in these sessions:

   (a) Interviews.
   (b) Dealing with work supervisors/work-mates.
   (c) Dealing with social agencies and bureaucrats.
   (d) Asking a friend to the house.
   (e) Asking a favour.
   (f) Going to a restaurant.
   (g) Approaching others at a party or discotheque.
   (h) Being short changed in a shop.
   (i) Disagreement with family.
   (j) Dealing with pushy shop assistants.
   (k) Telling someone your problems.
   (l) Listening to another person's problems.

4. *HOMEWORK*
   Individual work.

SESSION 12

INDIVIDUAL WORK AND GOODBYES

1. *NAME AND POSITIVE EVENT REPORT*

2. *HOMEWORK FEEDBACK*

3. *INDIVIDUAL ROLE-PLAYS*
   As in Sessions 10 and 11.

4. *THERAPISTS' GOODBYES*
   About half an hour before group is due to finish, therapists say goodbye and leave the group to decide on their own farewells and any
   future arrangements to meet.

7.2. INTRODUCTORY SOCIAL SKILLS TRAINING PROGRAMME FOR A MENTALLY HANDICAPPED POPULATION

Devised by Jim McDonald and John Flynn, charge nurses at Northfield Unit for the Mentally Handicapped, Aldershot.

This programme was designed for about six mentally handicapped adult residents to improve their social skills in specific situations which they are likely to encounter inside the unit and in the community.

The sessions last for one hour (including coffee) and the group meets with four staff members once a week. Other members of staff are involved in the homework assignments.

The programme includes an incentive scheme which has proved to be very popular with the group members. At the beginning of training each member is given a booklet in which he sticks a star which he is awarded for each session he attends. At the end of training he receives a £1 note for the full complement of stars. This can be spent in one of the local shops and the expedition forms an extension of training.

This introductory programme is followed by a further five sessions which include:

(a) Using the telephone inside the unit.
(b) Using the telephone outside.
(c) Going to a cafe.
(d) Going on a bus.
(e) Dressing and personal appearance.

SESSION 1

GREETINGS

1. *NAMES*
   Group sits round in a circle and each member tells his or her name to the others.

2. *EXPLANATION*
   Explain what we are going to do, what is expected of everyone and what rewards there will be.

3. *GAME*
   Dancing on squares or hoops. Hoops are placed on the floor. The group mills around the room. When the music stops each person stands in a hoop. The hoops are gradually removed until all the group is standing in one hoop.

4. *WARM-UP EXERCISE*
   Walk around to music. Stop. Say 'Hello' to somebody next to you. Repeat several times.

5. *INSTRUCTION AND MODELLING*
   The group leaders explain and demonstrate ways of greeting someone. They show a bad example first, then a good one. This could simply be meeting a friend in the street. Important behaviours are:

   (a) *Posture* — standing up straight at an appropriate distance.
   (b) *Gesture* — shaking hands or embracing.
   (c) *Facial expression* — smiling but not silly laughing.
   (d) *Verbal content* — 'Hello, how are you? It's nice to see you again. What have you been doing?' etc.

6. *ROLE-PLAY*

The above greetings are carried out by the group in pairs. They are asked to imagine they are meeting someone they know slightly in the gardens. Praise is given and, where necessary, guidance. Each pair can show their exercise to the group.

7. *GAME*

Repeat the Hoops Game above in order to finish off in a good mood.

8. *REWARD*

Refreshments and token for attending.

9. *HOMEWORK*

Initiated by Group Leaders meeting Residents on the bungalows.

SESSION 2

SHARING

1. *NAMES*
   Each member tells his name and the bungalow where he lives or works.

2. *HOMEWORK FEEDBACK*
   How did people get on with their greetings?

3. *WARM-UP EXERCISE* (Repeat practise from previous week)
   Following from exercise last week, we mill around the room, then stop and meet somebody, say 'Hello' and introduce ourselves, or say what we've been doing.

4. *GAME*
   Passing the parcel — or a variation. We are going to be passing things around in our exercise today.)

5. *INSTRUCTION AND MODELLING*
   (a) *Passing sweets around,* e.g. 'Would you like a sweet?', smiling and letting person choose his own. Person receiving says, 'Thank you' choosing only one and not a handful.
   (b) *Giving a present,* e.g. 'This is a present for your birthday, it's from all of us. I hope you like it.' Note gesture, the way the present is handed to the person, maybe shaking hands.
   (c) *Showing something of interest to someone else,* such as something they have bought in a shop. 'I've just bought this soap. Doesn't it smell nice?'

6. *ROLE-PLAY*
   The above 'sharing exercises' are repeated in appropriate situations by the groups in pairs. Praise is given and those in difficulty are guided through the different stages.

7. *GAME*
Repeat the Hoops Game from last week so everyone gets to know it.

8. *REWARD*
Refreshments and token.

9. *HOMEWORK*
The exercises are practised in real life with the help of the bungalow staff.

SESSION 3

BUYING AT A SHOP

1. *NAMES*
   Each member tells his name to the group. Note if there is now any more confidence.

2. *HOMEWORK FEEDBACK*
   How did people get on with the sharing experience?

3. *WARM-UP EXERCISE* (Repeat practise from previous session)
   Sitting in a circle, each member shows us something that he has bought. This could be clothing, a watch, jewellery.

4. *WARM-UP EXERCISE*
   Going around the circle again each member tells the group of something else he would like to buy.

5. *INSTRUCTION AND MODELLING*
   For example:
   'Good morning, I'd like to buy some shampoo.'
   'Which kind would you like?'
   'One for greasy hair.'
   'This is on special offer.'
   'How much is it?'
   Discussion about whether we handle the goods we buy, waiting in a queue, etc. Emphasize importance of verbal content, clarity of expression, gesture, facial expression.

6. *ROLE-PLAY*
   A shop attendant is chosen, then each person takes a turn at buying an article in a shop. Knowledge of money does not matter for this particular exercise, but they have to remember to wait for any change. Praise is given and any necessary guidance.

7. *GAME*
The group, with the exception of one member, forms a circle, holding hands. The 'outsider' has to break into the middle. Repeat several times. This should end the group on a good note.

8. *REWARD*
Refreshments and token.

9. *HOMEWORK*
Residents are sent to shops. Staff observe.

SESSION 4

ASKING FOR A DANCE

1. *NAMES*
   Each person tells his name to group, what bungalow he lives in and which shop he visited last week.

2. *HOMEWORK FEEDBACK*
   How did they get on at the shops? Do they feel any more confident? Do we need to practise this again?

3. *GAME*
   Passing the Orange. An orange is passed under chins along a line of people. This should break down physical barriers between people.

4. *WARM-UP EXERCISE*
   Milling around to music, music stops, each person finds a partner.
   (a) Pairs touch each other for 5 seconds (on the shoulders!).
   (b) Look each other in the eyes for 5 seconds.

5. *INSTRUCTION AND MODELLING*
   Sitting down on chairs, one gets up to ask the other for a dance, e.g.
   'Could I have the next dance with you?'
   'Will you dance with me?'
   'I would like to have a dance with you.'

6. *ROLE-PLAY*
   The above is practised in pairs. Praise is given and, where necessary, the person is guided through. Then finish with a dance when each one goes to ask his partner.

7. *GAME*
   At the group's request, a game that we have already played and know.

8. *REWARD*
Refreshments and token.

9. *HOMEWORK*
Going to a dance at one of the neighbouring hospitals.

SESSION 5

TAKING AND GIVING MESSAGES

1. *NAME*
   Group sits round in a circle and each member tells his or her name to the others.

2. *HOMEWORK FEEDBACK*
   How did everyone get on at the dance?

3. *GAME*
   Shoes in a bag. All take off their shoes and put them in a laundry bag. Then they mill around to music and when it stops each person has to find his own shoes and put them on as quickly as possible, making sure they are on the correct feet!

4. *WARM-UP EXERCISE*
   Round the circle list.

First person says to his neighbour:	'Can you buy me a packet of cigarettes?'
Second person says to his neighbour:	'Can you buy me a packet of cigarettes and a box of matches?'
Third person says to his neighbour:	'Can you buy me a packet of cigarettes, a box of matches and a newspaper?'

   Each person adding something on to the last.
   Perhaps two circles to make it easier.

5. *INSTRUCTION AND MODELLING*
   For example:
   'Will you go to the shop and ask for two pints of milk?'
   'Mr Jones would like two pints of milk, please.'

   'Will you go to the office and tell Mr Smith I will be coming at 4.30?'
   'Mr Jones asked me to tell you he will be coming at 4.30.'
   Emphasis on being clear and accurate, also on facial expression.

6. *ROLE-PLAY*

The above is practised in threes in different situations. Praise is given and the person guided if necessary.

7. *GAME*

Dancing in the hoops to finish on a good note.

8. *REWARD*

Refreshments and token.

9. *HOMEWORK*

Liaise with bungalows to let members of the group go on messages around the Unit.

7.3   WORK SOCIAL SKILLS PROGRAMME FOR REHABILITATION OF CHRONIC PSYCHIATRIC PATIENTS

Based on a programme originally designed by Frances D. O'Sullivan, clinical psychologist, Netherne Hospital, Surrey

The programme was designed to prepare people for applying for jobs, job interviews and being at work. It is part of a rehabilitation scheme for chronic patients, mostly schizophrenics, some of whom are nearing discharge from the hospital and others having already been discharged into the community. On average, the group consists of six members of mixed sexes and ages meeting for nine weekly sessions of 1½ hours. There are two therapists, one male and one female.

The programme has two important features. First, the majority of instruction is given in the form of detailed handouts, written in simple, plain English, each one covering a specific topic area, e.g. non-verbal communication or job applications. Each member of the group receives one handout a week in advance of the session in which those behaviours are to be practised. They are expected to familiarize themselves with the content of the handout which they can then discuss at the next session before proceeding on to the role-plays.

Secondly, the homework assignments are tied in with an individual and group incentive scheme. Each member of the group receives a homework handout (Figure 3) on which are listed the tasks to be practised that week. The first three items remain constant throughout the programme and new items relating to the theme of the session are added week by week. Each person is required to mark off on the handout the degree to which he is coping and the frequency of attempting the task. The therapist then works out the points earned by the patient by averaging the coping scores and multiplying this figure by the actual number of times the task has been carried out that week. The maximum number of points that could have been earned for each task (highest average coping score × highest frequency) can be entered in the last column. The total number of points earned by the patient are expressed as a percentage of the total maximum number of points that could have been earned. A target figure of 60 per cent is set for each member each week as the minimum he should attempt to achieve. The weekly percentage figure achieved is plotted on a progress chart which is used to monitor and feedback the weekly progress to the individual patient. The scores of all patients are combined into an average score, similarly plotted, to monitor and feedback to the group.

HOMEWORK HANDOUT FOR SESSION 2

NAME: Joan Hamble   DATE: w/c 4 July

O/P or I/P: O.P.

WARD/VILLA/UNIT (if I/P): Rehab

Weekly tasks	Coping level (5-1) 5 = very good 1 = very poor Day							Frequency (No. of times done in week)	Points earned	Max. points
	1	2	3	4	5	6	7			
1. Practise relaxation exercises morning and evening every day	4	5	4	5	5	5	5	1 2 3 4 5 6 7	35	35
2. Practise coping, positive self-talk before getting up	3	2	3	4	3	3	3	1 2 3 4 5 6 7	21	35
3. Check that personal appearance is as presentable as possible each morning	5	5	5	5	5	5	5	1 2 3 4 5 6 7	35	35
4. Practise walking confidently into a room (min. 5 times/day)	1	2	1	2	2	3	3	1 2 3 4 5 6 7	14	35
5. Practise sitting in a confident relaxed manner (min. 5 times/day)	1	2	1	2	3	3	3	1 2 3 4 5 6 7	14	35
6. Practise shaking hands with eye contact (min. 5 times/day)	3	3	3					1 2 3 4 5 6 7	9	35
7. Practise eye contact when talking and listening (min. 10 times/day)	3	3	4	3	4			1 2 3 4 5 6 7	15	35
8. Before going to sleep think of at least *one* positive event	5	5	5	5	5	5	5	1 2 3 4 5 6 7	35	35
Other difficult situations: 9.								1 2 3 4 5 6 7		
10.								1 2 3 4 5 6 7		
11.										
12.										

Percentage of maximum $= \dfrac{178}{280} \times 100 = 64\%$

Total weekly points: 178 280

COMMENTS ON MOOD AND EFFORT THIS WEEK:

TARGET WEEKLY PERCENTAGE: 60%   Signed: Joan Hamble

Figure 3.

SESSION 1

FAMILIARIZATION

Therapists introduce themselves to the group and then ask each group member in turn to introduce themselves.

Explain the rationale of the course and explain operant conditioning programme and how to work the homework sheets by demonstrating with examples on the blackboard. Emphasize the importance of doing the homework assignments every week for consolidation of learning as well as reading each handout before the next session to help understand the principles behind it.

Give out handout for Session 2 (Non-verbal communication particularly as related to job situation).

Emphasize the importance of group cohesiveness, i.e. commitment to the group as a whole rather than seeing themselves as a collection of individuals — punctuality and regularity of attendance essential, etc.

Answer queries.

SESSION 2

SHOWING CONFIDENCE

1. Apologies for absence last week.

2. Reinforce starting on time and level of attendance, if applicable.

3. Positive event reporting from each group member.

4. Explain briefly the principles of anxiety management (reciprocal inhibition) and discuss useful brief exercises such as deep breathing, coping self-talk (talking oneself *into* something rather than *out* of it), importance of non-avoidance of anxiety-provoking situations. Give handouts for relaxation exercises (complete version).

5. *INSTRUCTION*
   Any queries from last week's handout on non-verbal communication? Brief discussion if necessary. Introduce use of eye contact and posture to give confident manner and stress the importance of this in the first 2-3 minutes of an interview.

6. *ROLE-PLAY*
   Each member practises, as if at an interview, coming into the room in a confident manner, shaking hands with eye contact and sitting down in a relaxed, confident manner in front of the interviewer after appropriate modelling by the therapists. No words spoken apart from time of day greeting and self-introduction. Group feedback for each performance.

7. Brief discussion on how one can 'give oneself away' or project an air of confidence *before* a word is said. This is vital in setting up a positive atmosphere from the start of an interview. If you behave confidently you will feel more confident.

8. *HOMEWORK HANDOUT*
   Homework handout sheet (see example) is given out together with operant conditioning therapy handout for guidance.

9. *INSTRUCTION HANDOUT*
   Instruction handout for next week's session given out (Vocal expression).

10. Thanks for attendance. Close group session.

SESSION 3

VOCAL EXPRESSION

1. Explanations for any absences last week.

2. Reinforce starting on time and level of attendance, if applicable.

3. Positive event reporting from each group member.

4. *HOMEWORK FEEDBACK*
    Homework sheets collected. Feedback — deal with any queries/ problems. For example, did they manage to relax properly? Give handout of *short* relaxation exercises.

5. *INSTRUCTION*
    Any queries from last week's handout on vocal expression? Discussion of the importance of voice cues in communication.

6. *WARM-UP EXERCISE*
    Give rationale, provide model for group and then in pairs, each person takes it in turn to recite numbers in different ways to express different emotions, e.g. anger, excitement, depression, interest, boredom, friendliness, etc.

7. *ROLE-PLAY*
    At work in the coffee break one person reading items of news to another. Therapist models reading a short newspaper item once badly and then appropriately with suitable expression. Each member of the group reads the item of news provided to the others trying to convey the appropriate emotion and emphasis. Group give feedback on clarity, tone, pitch and speed.

8. Short open discussion of the points raised and learnt from exercises and role-playing.

9. *HOMEWORK HANDOUT*
   In addition to practising the relaxation tasks, etc. each member has to select an item from the newspaper each day and practise reading it aloud, putting in the appropriate emphasis and tone, etc. If possible members would benefit from recording it on tape and listening to the playback to give extra feedback, otherwise they will have to have the co-operation of a relative or friend as a critical listener.

10. *INSTRUCTION HANDOUT*
    Instruction handout for Session 4 given out (Conversation — opening, maintaining and closing).

11. Thanks for attendance. Close group session.

12. *INDIVIDUAL FEEDBACK*
    Private feedback on previous week's homework given to each member.

SESSION 4

CONVERSATION

1. Explanations of absences.

2. Reinforce starting on time and level of attendance, if applicable.

3. Positive event reporting by each member of group in turn.

4. *HOMEWORK FEEDBACK*
   Homework sheets collected. How did everyone get on? Answer any queries and deal with any problems arising from homework.

5. *INSTRUCTION*
   Queries from last week's handout on starting, maintaining and ending conversations. Discussion of starting conversations in the canteen at work.

6. *ROLE-PLAY*
   In the canteen at work. One person joins a table with others at it and starts a conversation with the person next to him. Modelled by therapist followed by each member of the group taking a turn in initiating conversation. Feedback on appropriateness of opening remark and vocal expression.

7. *INSTRUCTION*
   Discussion of listening, speaking and taking turns in conversation.

8. *ROLE-PLAY*
   Previous situation, but with conversation continuing for one minute. Modelled first by therapist.

9. *INSTRUCTION*
   Discussion on ending conversations.

10. *ROLE-PLAY*
    Previous role-play which is brought to an appropriate end. Modelled and then each member taking it in turns.

11. Short discussion on the points learned from the role-plays on conversation.

12. *HOMEWORK HANDOUT*
    Each member is to initiate and hold a conversation with another person at least once each day.

13. *INSTRUCTION HANDOUT*
    Instruction handout for Session 5 given out (Job applications). Notes on telephone and letter applications as well as a sample application form to complete with instructions on how to do so.

14. Thanks for attendance. Close group session.

15. *INDIVIDUAL FEEDBACK*
    Private feedback on previous week's homework given to each member.

SESSION 5

APPLYING FOR A JOB

1. Explanations of any absences.

2. Reinforce starting on time and level of attendance, if applicable.

3. Positive event reporting by each member of the group in turn.

4. *HOMEWORK FEEDBACK*
   Give names of those who achieved their target percentages last week but do not mention any figures. Hand out individual graphs and read out group average. Encourage those who did badly last week to make more effort this week. Answer any queries and deal with any problems arising from homework last week. Emphasize the importance of doing the homework if progress is to be made and consolidated.

5. *INSTRUCTION*
   Any problems/queries from last week's handout? Brief discussion if necessary.

6. *ROLE-PLAY*
   Using internal phone and tape-recorder, model telephoning for an application form/interview appointment — first badly with feedback from the group and then appropriately with positive and negative feedback from the group, on
   (a) clarity,
   (b) confidence,
   (c) brevity but with politeness,
   (d) overall air of efficiency and competence.

   Each member of the group then takes it in turn to role-play telephoning
   (a) for an application form if post is still vacant,
   (b) for an interview appointment.

7. Short discussion of the points raised and learnt from *experience* as well as from exercises.

8. Collection of graph sheets for recording this week's figures. Group graph to be pinned on the wall. Emphasize that effort is needed from *everyone* in order not to let the group down.

9. *HOMEWORK HANDOUT*
   Practise writing 'dummy' letter for application form/interview.

10. *INSTRUCTION HANDOUT*
    Distribute instruction handout for Session 6 (Job interviews).

11. Thanks for attendance. Close group session.

12. *INDIVIDUAL FEEDBACK*
    Private feedback on previous week's homework given to each member.

SESSIONS 6 AND 7

JOB INTERVIEWS

1. Explanations for any absences.

2. Reinforce starting on time and level of attendance, if applicable.

3. Positive event reporting by each member.

4. Collection of last week's homework sheets.

5. *HOMEWORK FEEDBACK*
   Those members who achieved the target percentage last week (or above the target figure) are reinforced with praise. Others need to make a more *consistent* effort by finding a sympathetic relative or friend to practise role-playing sessions/exercises, etc. (Individual feedback at the end of the group.)

6. Group average graph. Pin the chart on the wall and indicate with drawing pins and coloured rubber bands where the group is at in its progress. (Take it down at the end of the session.)

7. *INSTRUCTION*
   Any queries/problems with last week's handout on technique of job interviews? Brief discussion if necessary.

8. *ROLE-PLAY*
   (a) Bad models of how *not* to behave at interviews — i.e.
       (i) too timid,
       (ii) too aggressive and cocky.

(b) Good model, demonstrating the following characteristics:
  (i) quiet confidence,
  (ii) politeness combined with businesslike approach,
  (iii) interest (eye contact): listening skills as well as ability to talk.
  (iv) knowing when to end the interview and appropriate leave-taking.

Half the group to role-play being an interviewee with positive and negative feedback from the rest of the group.

Ask if any members would like to role-play the boss to know what it feels like to be on the other side of the fence.

9. Discussion with the half of the group who have been role-playing of any real-life interviews they have had and what they have learnt from them.

10. *HOMEWORK HANDOUT* (For the next two weeks: answer any queries arising)
Homework handout given for the next two weeks. Includes consolidation of previously learned skills plus constructing and rehearsing a list of positive assets an employer could be offered.

11. *INSTRUCTION HANDOUT*
No further instruction handout for Session 7 (Job interview technique). Other half of the group who have not taken part in the role-play this week to be prepared to role-play mock interviews in the next session. In Session 6 handout for Session 8 (Assertive behaviour, concerned with expressing feelings, first day at work, dealing with an unsympathetic boss or workmate and refusing unreasonable requests).

12. Thanks for attendance. Close group session.

13. *INDIVIDUAL FEEDBACK*
Private feedback on previous week's homework given to each member.

SESSION 8

ASSERTIVE BEHAVIOUR

1. Explanations for any absences.

2. Reinforce starting on time and level of attendance, if applicable.

3. Positive event reporting by each member.

4. Collection of last week's homework sheets.

5. *HOMEWORK FEEDBACK*
   Refer to group average graph, and give feedback.

6. *INSTRUCTION*
   Any queries/problems from last week's handout?
   Discussion on last week's handout as it applies to everyday situations, e.g. complaining about cold food in a canteen/restaurant; taking a defective article back to a shop; correcting someone when they misrepresent what you have said or else have given false information, etc.

7. *ROLE-PLAY* (Time for *good* models only)
   Model how to cope with the following:
   (a) *Refusing an unreasonable request* (e.g. refusing to work through the lunch-hour when it is not an unavoidable emergency but is caused by the inefficiency of another staff member).
   (b) *An aggressive foreman/supervisor* (e.g. refusing to accept your reasonable excuse for being late or else getting impatient when you ask a second time how to carry out a task).
   (c) *Taking a defective article back to a shop* (e.g. faulty shoes, etc.).
   (d) *Sending back a cold or unsatisfactory meal in a canteen/restaurant.*
   Get the group in turn to pair with one of the therapists and practise any one of the above situations.

8. *HOMEWORK HANDOUT*
   Practise assertive behaviour including positive assertion of opinion, making decisions and refusing an unreasonable request (if applicable).

9. *INSTRUCTION HANDOUT*
   Distribute instruction handout for Session 9.

10. Information about the final session next week. There will be no role-playing. The session will consist of answering queries about the tax handout, working out a model weekly budget on the blackboard, post-treatment assessment questionnaires and filling in feedback questionnaire on the course followed by final homework feedback to each individual group member in turn.

11. Thanks for attendance. Close group session.

12. *INDIVIDUAL FEEDBACK*
    Private feedback on previous week's homework given to each member.

SESSION 9

MONEY MANAGEMENT

1. Explanations of any absences.

2. Positive event reporting by each group member.

3. Homework feedback. Draw attention to group average on chart. Need for *everyone* to carry out their homework assignments.

4. Welcome tax adviser. Discussion about last week's handout. Tax adviser available to answer any queries or problems arising therefrom. Handouts to be given to any members absent last week.

5. Give out new handout on weekly budgeting. When every member has read the handout discuss it and answer any queries arising.

6. Post-treatment assessment.

7. Ask each member in turn what they thought was the most significant thing they got out of attending the group.

8. Thanks for attendance and close the group session.

9. Individual homework feedback for each member of the group.

7.4 AGGRESSION MANAGEMENT PROGRAMME FOR YOUNG OFFENDERS IN CUSTODY

Developed from a programme devised by Adrian Neil and Christine Curle, prison psychologists, Portland Borstal.

The programme consists of eight weekly sessions, each lasting approximately 2 hours. It was designed for six or seven borstal trainees (young male adult offenders) and two trainers.

The trainees selected for the programme had frequently been in trouble for aggressive behaviour in the borstal and also might have acted violently outside the institution, although they had not necessarily been convicted of offences involving violence. The programme aims to teach alternative strategies of behaviour which can be applied to a variety of situations; individual training in relaxation and tension control as related to loss of temper and aggression can be undertaken at the same time.

SESSION 1

INTRODUCTION

1. *INTRODUCTION*
   Co-leaders introduce themselves to the rest of the group and ask members to do the same.

   Explain *rules* of the group:
   (a) no physical violence,
   (b) freedom of expression and confidentiality of what is said in the group,
   (c) the phrase 'I can't' is not allowed in the group; everyone is expected to try things out.

   Discuss the need to look *in detail* at situations which cause anger and loss of temper and how the group can help by sharing common experiences and finding solutions.

   Explain that the group requires active involvement and uses *role-play* to try out different ways of behaving in order to see what their effects are.

   Stress the importance of *practising* what is learnt in each session during the rest of the week and say that each following session will start with *feedback* about how members have been getting on.

2. *INSTRUCTION*
   'When violence occurs it is almost always the result of interpersonal situations getting out of hand — it hardly ever arises out of the blue. The purpose of the group is to look at how this may occur and to work out better ways of handling problems or minor disputes so that the situations don't build up until the only possible outcome is violence.'

   Look at different ways of handling potentially violent situations. Model submissive, aggressive and assertive behaviours in this type of situation. Get the group to identify components of assertive responses in terms of non-verbal and verbal behaviours.

3. *PRACTICE* (Homework)
   (a) Observe someone behaving too aggressively or too submissively. What is it that gives that impression?
   (b) Fill in on the sheet problem situations (Figure 4) that have occurred recently (e.g. within the past two years). Give as many details as possible. Bring them back to discuss next week.

PROBLEM SITUATION SHEET

Where?

When?

Who else was involved?

What happened?

Figure 4.

SESSION 2

HOW VIOLENCE HAPPENS — 'DEFUSING' A POTENTIALLY VIOLENT SITUATION

1. *INTRODUCTION*

   Reinforce members for attendance (indicates that they have not been in serious trouble since the last session).

   Feedback of events in the past week. Each member reports on incidents, particularly those involving potential or actual violence, and how they handled them. Other members (or co-leaders) make comments or suggestions for alternative behaviours.

   Practice reports. Check that members have completed the problem situation forms and help with any difficulties.

2. *INSTRUCTION*

   Get each member to read out what he has written on his form. Others can ask for further details or clarification. Common themes (i.e. factors which trigger off violence or loss of control) are written up on a blackboard.

   'Why do people become involved in violent situations?' Draw out possible reasons, referring to common themes already recorded, e.g. gaining a reputation as a 'hard man', defending a reputation, self-defence (seeing other people as dangerous), getting rid of pressures or tension, bullying (gaining pleasure from violence), exploitation (using it as a means to an end).

   Some of the themes are role-played by the group (as they happened but stopping short of physical violence!). Situations are taken from the forms or from recent events in the borstal (e.g. being unable to back down from a challenge or losing face in front of mates).

   Identify non-verbal signs of aggression (facial expression, posture, gestures) verbal behaviour (provocative words which lead to escalation rather than cooling the situation). Discussion of the consequences of violence and alternative strategies to prevent those situations becoming violent.

3. *ROLE-PLAY*

   Situation. The same themes are taken again, but this time handled in a non-aggressive manner.

   Procedure. Role-play in sub-groups, if necessary practising in a corner of the room before repeating in front of the rest of the group. Co-leaders help out or initiate as appropriate. Feedback from members not involved in each scene and from video.

4. *PRACTICE*

   (a) Observe the sort of 'violence behaviours' you and other people engage in. Report back next week on some situations and how they built up.

   (b) If situations you are in seem likely to 'blow up', practise new behaviours to diffuse the situation.

SESSION 3

DEALING WITH CRITICISM

1. *INTRODUCTION*
   Reinforce members for getting to the group.
   Feedback of incidents in past week.
   Practice reports.

2. *INSTRUCTION*
   'Criticism is a normal part of life (e.g. your parents get on at you for being unemployed/in trouble; the boss calls you in to talk about being late; you are being blamed for something which was not your fault). If the situation isn't handled properly it may make you over-react and feel provoked into violence (either verbal or physical).'

   Elicit from the group the usual ways of dealing with criticism — denial, defensiveness, retaliation. 'The trouble is these just lead to arguments which drag on or build up and, if neither side will back down, the situation can get out of hand.'

   Explore how criticism usually makes a person *feel* — anxious, angry or guilty. 'Consequently, you will not behave in a calm or confident way, you may say or do the wrong thing or get stuck for words. In any case, you probably will not learn from your mistakes, will put people off or put yourselves down.'

   'If criticism is *fair*, it's best to get matters out in the open, to accept and acknowledge it by agreeing and coming to some workable compromise. Likewise, if the criticism is unfair, instead of reacting in a negative way, it is better to discuss it openly and calmly, trying to distinguish fact from opinion and feeling.'

   Model to show that it is possible to agree with whatever truth there is in the criticism without being submissive; also, how manipulative criticism can be extinguished by drawing it out into the open.

3. *ROLE-PLAY*

   Situation. Being criticized fairly then unfairly by staff and then by peers.

   Procedure. Practised in pairs and presented to the group for feedback.

4. *PRACTICE*

   (a) Observe how other people deal with criticism — what are the consequences?

   (b) Practise dealing with criticism — how does it work out?

SESSION 4

MAKING REQUESTS AND TAKING ORDERS

1. *INTRODUCTION*
   Reinforce members for attendance.
   Feedback of incidents in past week.
   Practice reports.

2. *INSTRUCTION I* (Making requests)
   Focus on those situations where someone is standing in the way of
   what you want, e.g. asking someone to move a car which is blocking
   a pub car park; asking someone to turn down the volume on a record
   player; asking someone in a phone box to hurry up. Discuss and elicit
   from the group various ways of handling these situations (and their
   respective outcomes) in terms of assertive rather than aggressive
   behaviour, e.g. firm tone of voice, looking the other in the eye, clear
   verbal message. Model.

3. *ROLE-PLAY*
   Situation. Members choose from a previously drawn up list of
   situations in which assertive behaviour is appropriate.
   Procedure. Practised in pairs and presented to the group for
   feedback.

4. *INSTRUCTION II* (Accepting orders)
   Elicit from group types of situation. 'It is essential to be able to
   identify those situations in which it is important to accept and carry
   out the order without questioning because any other action would
   lead to undesired consequences, such as dismissal or loss of privi-
   leges. In other situations, where the order is unreasonable or for
   some reason the person may be unable to carry out the order, it may
   be necessary to engage in negotiation.' Discuss verbal and non-verbal
   responses in these situations and model appropriate responses.

5. *ROLE-PLAY*
   Situations
   (a) Being given an order at work where it is important to comply
       even though you don't want to.

(b) Being told to do a job when it's your lunch break.

Procedure. Practised in pairs and presented to the group for feedback.

6. *PRACTICE*

    (a) Observe how other people make requests. Practise making requests as suggested; pay particular attention to the outcome.

    (b) Practise accepting orders in a way which is neither aggressive nor submissive.

SESSION 5

PEER GROUP PRESSURE

1. *INTRODUCTION*
   Reinforce members for getting to the group.
   Feedback from events of the past week.
   Practice reports.

2. *INSTRUCTION I* (Saying no)
   'Others can sometimes put pressure on you to do things that you don't necessarily want to do and which may get you into trouble, e.g. your mates are out looking for a fight but you've just come out of borstal and don't want trouble. Look at the ways people put pressure on — calling you a coward, a lousy friend, pointing out the benefits but not the bad consequences such as getting caught. Saying no involves standing up for yourself without getting into a fight or crawling away.' Discuss the behaviours involved.

3. *ROLE-PLAY*
   Situation. Group members identify situations involving peer group pressure either from the past or which are likely to occur when they get outside.
   Procedure. Set up in small groups, practised and presented to whole group for feedback.

4. *INSTRUCTION II* (Teasing)
   Discussion with group about teasing, why people do it, how it makes the person feel, how he reacts, and how these situations can escalate into violence. Usually the person does it to get a reaction, and if he gets it he has 'won'. Look at appropriate ways of responding so that the person does not feel the other has got the better of him, such as ignoring the person or his remarks, avoiding provocative language, leaving the situation, making a joke.

5. *ROLE-PLAY*

   Situation. Being teased by peers, situations selected by individuals.

   Procedure. Practised in twos or threes and presented to the group for feedback.

6. *PRACTICE*

   (a) Identify situations where you feel under pressure from your peers to do something you don't really want to do. Practise saying no.

   (b) If you are being teased, try suggested behaviours.

SESSIONS 6, 7 AND 8

These sessions are devoted to individual work on any of the members' specific difficulties, or some of the following themes might be taken as appropriate.

ROLE PLAYS FOR NON-AGGRESSIVE BEHAVIOUR

Problems at home (Family or girlfriend)
1. Girlfriend/wife stays out without saying where she is.
2. Your brother has broken something of yours.
3. You arrive home drunk.
4. Your girl friend has been seen out with another bloke.
5. Another bloke has been bothering your girl friend.
6. Your parents get on at you for being unemployed/in trouble.
7. Your parents don't like your girl/wife.

Problems at work
1. Workmate makes fun of you.
2. Boss or supervisor gives you orders.
3. Boss calls you in to talk about being late.
4. There has been an accident at work which isn't your fault and the boss blames you.

Problems with friends
1. Your mates are out looking for a fight, but you've just come out of borstal and don't want trouble.
2. Your mate gets into a fight in a pub.
3. You are stopped from getting into a club by the bouncer.
4. One of the 'chaps' in your town has heard that you've just got out of borstal and wants to see how 'tasty' you are.

Problems in borstal
1. Taking orders from a young officer.
2. Making a request from an officer, for example asking for a letter or about your board.
3. Being wound up by other trainees in the house.

Problems with the police
1. Told to move on by a policeman when arguing with a friend in the street.

2. Stopped by the police when driving.
3. Stopped by police in the street.

If the situation is relevant to the whole group then the procedure is the same as in previous sessions, i.e. instructions are given and the members practise before presenting to the group for feedback. If it is a problem for just one individual, the group can be involved in providing suggestions and setting the scene. Practice should be related to each session.

7.5 HETEROSOCIAL SKILLS TRAINING PROGRAMME FOR A SHY MALE

Based on a programme devised by Andrea Edeleanu, clinical psychologist, Brookwood Hospital.

These sessions were originally developed as part of a psychotherapeutic programme for a 22-year-old man. The aim of the sessions was to provide him with the skills to help him develop his relationship with a female colleague with whom he played squash once a week.

The training was carried out on a one-to-one basis in five sessions of approximately half an hour held at fortnightly intervals.

Although the trainer would have a general outline of such a programme before training commenced, the details of each session would be worked out as training progressed so as to be relevant to the particular circumstances at the time.

SESSION 1

DEVELOPING THE RELATIONSHIP

1. *INSTRUCTION*
   Expressing interest/affection through posture, facial expression, tone of voice, eye contact, gesture and discrete touch and checking out her reaction. Model.

2. *ROLE-PLAY*
   After squash game, coming out of court hand on her shoulder, looking at her, congratulate or commiserate affectionately.

3. *HOMEWORK*
   Repeat role-play in vivo.

SESSION 2

ASKING OUT AND BEING ON A DATE

1. *INSTRUCTION I* (Asking out)

   Discuss various ways of asking her out, e.g. checking out the kind of activities she enjoys before actually asking, asking directly, asking her to join him with other friends in a pub. Stress getting the message clear and warm tone of voice. Discuss recovery strategies if she says 'no'.

2. *ROLE-PLAY*

   As previous week, this time adding 'There's a good film on at the Odeon next week, would you like to go one evening?'

3. *INSTRUCTION II* (After the film)

   Discuss ways of developing the conversation from general to more personal topics. Self-disclosure of feelings. Observing the other's reaction and judging how self-disclosure is received.

4. *ROLE-PLAY*

   After the film. Taking about self. Expressing a liking for her company and a wish to get to know her better. Arrange another meeting.

5. *HOMEWORK*

   Practise role-plays in vivo.

SESSION 3

*EXPRESSION OF PHYSICAL ATTRACTION: DEVELOPING
A SEXUAL RELATIONSHIP*

1. *INSTRUCTION*
   Using visual materials and modelling discuss developing the physical aspects of the relationship; kissing and fondling, leading to more intimate exploration. No role-play this session!

2. *HOMEWORK*
   On next date say goodnight with a kiss and light embrace.

SESSION 4

BECOMING MORE INTIMATE

1. *INSTRUCTION*
   Discussion about developing the relationship further through conversation. For example, talking about feelings for the other person, what they enjoy about the relationship, views about other relationships, past experience, sex and contraception as well as sharing attitudes about matters of personal importance.

2. *ROLE-PLAY*
   On a date, in a quiet corner of a pub, tell her how much he is enjoying her company and how good she makes him feel.

3. *HOMEWORK*
   Practise role-play in vivo.

SESSION 5

CONSOLIDATING THE RELATIONSHIP

1. *INSTRUCTION*
   Discussion about agreeing on the nature of the relationship, how much time to spend together, likes and dislikes about each other, giving support and encouragement, being open and frank, dealing with arguments and criticism and making compromises.

2. *ROLE-PLAY 1*
   Girlfriend criticizes you for spending too much time with your friends who she doesn't particularly like.

   ROLE-PLAY 2
   You want to watch the match on television, she wants to go to the cinema.

   ROLE-PLAY 3
   She has had a disappointment (not got promotion) and is feeling low.

3. *HOMEWORK*
   Practise as appropriate.

References

Addington, D.W. (1968). 'The relationship of selected vocal characteristics to personality perception', *Speech Monographs*, **35**, 492-503.

Agras, W.S. (1972). *Behaviour Modification*, Boston, Little, Brown & Co.

Alberti, R.E. and Emmons, M.L. (1974). *Your Perfect Right: A Guide to Assertive Behaviour*, San Luis Obispo, California, Impact.

Annett, J. (1969). *Feedback and Human Behaviour*, Harmondsworth, Penguin.

Argyle, M. (1969). *Social Interaction*, London, Methuen.

Argyle, M. (1972). *The Psychology of Interpersonal Behaviour*, 2nd edn, Harmondsworth, Penguin.

Argyle, M. (1975). *Bodily Communication*, London, Methuen.

Argyle, M. and Cook, M. (1976). *Gaze and Mutual Gaze*, Cambridge, Cambridge University Press.

Argyris, C. (1965). 'Explorations in interpersonal competence. I', *Journal of Applied Behavioural Science*, **1**, 58-83.

Argyris, C. (1968). 'Conditions for competence acquisition and therapy', *Journal of Applied Behavioural Science*, **4**, 147-177.

Bandura, A. (1969). *Principals of Behaviour Modification*, New York, Holt, Rinehart and Winston.

Bandura, A. (1977). *Social Learning Theory*, New Jersey, Prentice-Hall.

Bandura, A., Grusec, J.D. and Menlove, F.L. (1967). 'Vicarious extinction of avoidance behaviour', *Journal of Personality and Social Psychology*, **5**, 16-23.

Barbee, J.R. and Keil, E.C. (1973). 'Experimental techniques of job interview training for the disadvantaged: Videotape feedback behaviour modification and microcounseling', *Journal of Applied Psychology*, **58**, 202-213.

Barker, L. (1971). *Listening Behaviour*, New Jersey, Prentice-Hall.

Beck, A.T., Rush, A.J., Shaw, B.F. and Emery, G. (1980). *Cognitive Therapy of Depression*, New York, Wiley.

Bellack, A.S. and Hersen, M. (1980). *Research and Practice in Social Skills Training*, New York and London, Plenum Press.

Bryant, B. and Trower, P.E. (1974). 'Social difficulty in a student sample', *British Journal of Educational Psychology*, **44**, 13-21.

Canter, S. and Wilkinson, J. (1978). *Social Skills Training Manual*, unpublished manual, University of Surrey, Guildford.

Cook, M. (1969). 'Anxiety, speech disturbances and speech rate, *British Journal of Social and Clinical Psychology*, **8**, 13-21.

Curran, J.P. (1977). 'Skills training as an approach to the treatment of hetero-sexual-social anxiety: A review', *Psychological Bulletin*, **84,** 140-157

Doty, D.W. (1975). 'Role-playing and incentives in the modification of the social interaction of chronic psychiatric patients', *Journal of Consulting and Clinical Psychology, 43,* 676-682.

Duncan, S. (1972). 'Some signals and rules for taking speaking turns in conversations, *Journal of Personality and Social Psychology, 23,* 283-292.

Duncan, S. and Fiske, D.W. (1977). *Face to Face Interaction: Research Method and Theory,* Hillsdale, New Jersey, Erlbaum.

Edelstein, B.A. and Eisler, R.M. (1976). 'Effects of modeling and modeling with feedback on the behavioral components of social skill', *Behaviour Therapy, 7,* 382-389.

Eisler, R.M., Blanchard, E.B. Fitts, H. and Williams, J.G. (1978). 'Social skill training with and without modeling on schizophrenic and non-psychotic hospitalized psychiatric patients', *Behaviour Modification, 2,* 147-172.

Eisler, R.M., Miller, P.M. and Hersen, M. (1973). 'Components of assertive behaviour', *Journal of Clinical Psychology, 29,* 295-299

Ekman, P. and Friesen, W.V. (1967). 'Head and body cues in the judgement of emotion: A reformulation, *Perceptual and Motor Skills, 24,* 179-215.

Ekman, P. and Friesen, W.V. (1969). 'Non-verbal leakage and clues to deception, *Psychiatry, 32,* 88-106.

Ekman, P. and Friesen, W.V. (1975). *Unmasking the Face,* Englewood Cliffs, New Jersey, Prentice-Hall.

Ekman, P., Friesen, W.V. and Ellsworth, P. (1972). *Emotion in the Human Face; Guidelines for Research and Integration of the Findings,* New York, Pergamon Press.

Eldred, S.H. and Price, D.B. (1958). 'Linguistic evaluation of feeling states in psychotherapy', *Psychiatry, 21,* 115-121.

Ellis, A. (1971). *Growth through Reason,* Palo Alto, California, Science and Behaviour Book.

Ervin-Tripp, S. (1973). 'An analysis of the interaction of language, topic and listener', in *Social Encounters* (Ed. M. Argyle) Harmondsworth, Penguin.

Gambrill, E.D. and Richey, C.A. (1975). 'An assertion inventory for use in assessment and research', *Behaviour Therapy, 6,* 550-561.

Goldfried, M.R. (1977). 'The use of relaxation and cognitive restructuring as coping skills' in *Behavioural Self-Management* (Ed. R.B. Stuart) New York, Brunner/Mazel.

Goldfried, M.R. and D'Zurilla, T.J. (1969). 'A behaviour-analytical model for assessing competence', in *Current Topics in Clinical and Community Psychology,* Vol. 1 (Ed. C.D. Speilberger) New York, Academic Press.

Goldsmith, J.B. and McFall, R.M. (1975). 'Development and evaluation of an interpersonal skill-training program for psychiatric patients', *Journal of Abnormal Psychology,* **84,** 51-58.

Hall, E.T. (1966). *The Hidden Dimension,* Garden City, New York, Doubleday.

Hersen, M. and Bellack, A.S. (1977). 'Assessment of social skills', in *Handbook of Behavioural Assessment* (Eds. A.R. Ciminero, K.S. Calhoun and H.E. Adams), New York, Wiley.

Jourard, S.M. (1966). 'An exploratory study of body accessibility', *British Journal of Social and Clinical Psychology, 5,* 221-231.

Kanfer, F.H. and Karoly, P. (1972). 'Self-control: A behaviouristic excursion into the lion's den', *Behaviour Therapy*, **3,** 398-418.

Kefgen, M. and Touchie-Specht, P. (1971). *Individuality in Clothing Selection and Personal Appearance. A Guide for the Consumer,* New York, Macmillan.

Kendon, A. (1967). 'Some functions of gaze direction in social interaction', *Acta Psychologica*, **26,** 1-47.

Kendon, A. (1973). 'The role of visible behaviour in the organisation of social interaction', in *Social Communication and Movement* (Eds. M. Von Cranach and I. Vine), London, Academic Press.

Lazarus, A.A. (1973). 'On assertive behaviour: A brief note', *Behaviour Therapy*, **4,** 697-699.

Leavitt, H.J. and Mueller, H.H. (1968). 'Some effects of feedback on communication', in *Interpersonal Communication: Survey and Studies,* (Ed. D. Barnlund), Boston, Houghton Mifflin.

Liberman, R.P., King, L.W., De Risi, W.J. and McCann, M. (1975). *Personal Effectiveness,* Illinois, Research Press.

Libet, J. and Lewinsohn, P.M. (1973). 'The concept of social skill with special references to the behaviour of depressed persons', *Journal of Consulting and Clinical Psychology,* **40,** 304-312.

Linehan, M.M., Goldfried, M.R. and Goldfried, A.P. (1979). 'Assertion therapy: Skill training or cognitive restructuring', *Behaviour Therapy*, **10,** 372-388.

McFall, R.M. and Marston, A.R. (1970). 'An experimental investigation of behaviour rehearsal in assertive training', *Journal of Abnormal Psychology*, **76,** 295-303.

McFall, R.M. and Twentyman, C.T. (1973). 'Four experiments on the relative contributions of rehearsal, modeling and coaching to assertive training', *Journal of Abnormal Psychology*, **81,** 199-218.

Marzillier, J.S. and Winter, K. (1978). 'Success and failure in social skills training: Individual differences', *Behaviour Research and Therapy*, **16,** 67-84.

Marzillier, J.S., Lambert, C. and Kellett, J. (1976). 'A controlled evaluation of systematic desensitization and social skills training for socially inadequate psychiatric patients', *Behaviour Research and Therapy*, **14,** 225-238.

Mehrabian, A. (1968). 'The inference of attitudes from the posture, orientation and distance of a communication', *Journal of Consulting Psychology*, **32,** 296-308.

Mehrabian, A. (1971). *Silent Messages,* Belmon, California, Wadsworth Publications Co. Inc.

Mehrabian, A. (1972). *Non-verbal Communication,* Chicago, Aldine Atherton.

Meichenbaum, D. (1974). *Cognitive Behaviour Modification,* Morristown, New Jersey, General Learning Press.

Percell, L.P., Berwick, P.T. and Biegel, A. (1974). 'The effects of assertive training on self-concept and anxiety', *Archives of General Psychiatry*, **31,** 502-504.

Pfeiffer, J.W. and Jones, J.E. (1979). *Handbook of Structured Experiences for Human Relations Training.* California, University Associates.

Porter, E., Argyle, M. and Salter, V. (1970). 'What is signalled by proximity?', *Psychological Bulletin*, **64,** 23-51.

Rahaim, S., Lefebvre, C. and Jenkins, J.O. (1980). 'The effects of social skills training on behavioural and cognitive components of anger management', *Journal of Behaviour Therapy and Experimental Psychiatry*, **11,** 3-8.

Rathus, S.A. (1973). 'A 30-item schedule for assessing assertive behaviour', *Behaviour Therapy,* **4,** 398-406.

Rimm, D.C., Hill, G.A., Brown, N.M. and Stuart, J.E. (1974). 'Group-assertiveness training in treatment of expression of inappropriate anger', *Psychological Reports,* **34,** 791-798.

Shepherd, G. (1977). 'Social skills training; The generalization problem', *Behaviour Therapy,* **8,** 1008-1009.

Shepherd, G. (1978). 'Social skills training: The generalization problem — some further data', *Behaviour Research and Therapy,* **16,** 287-288.

Skinner, B.F. (1953). *Science and Human Behaviour,* New York, Macmillan.

Sloan, R.B., Staples, F.R. Cristol, A.H., Yorkston, N.J. and Whipple, K. (1975). *Psychotherapy versus Behaviour Therapy,* Cambridge, Harvard University Press.

Spence, A.J. and Spence S.H. (1980). 'Cognitive changes associated with social skills training', *Behaviour Research and Therapy,* **18,** 265-272.

Strongman, K.T. and Champness, B.G. (1968). 'Dominance hierarchies and conflict in eye contact', *Acta Psychologica,* **28,** 376-386.

Trower, P.E., Bryant, B. and Argyle, M. (1978). *Social Skills and Mental Health,* London, Methuen.

Trower, P.E., Yardley, K.M., Bryant, B.M. and Shaw, P.H. (1978). 'The treatment of social failure: A comparison of anxiety-reduction and skills acquisition procedures on two social problems', *Behaviour Modification,* **2,** 41-60.

Tustin, A. (1966). 'Feedback', in *Communication and Culture* (Ed. A.G. Smith) New York, Holt, Rinehart and Winston.

Twentyman, G.T. and McFall, R.M. (1975). 'Behavioral training of social skills in shy males', *Journal of Consulting and Clinical Psychology,* **43,** 384-395.

Twentyman, C.T. and Martin, B. (1978). 'Modification of problem interaction in mother-child dyads by modeling and behavior rehearsal', *Journal of Clinical Psychology,* **34,** 138-143.

Wallace, C.J. (1980). *The Social Skills Training Project,* unpublished report, The Mental Health Clinical Research Centre for the Study of Schizophrenia, Camarillo, California.

Wallace, C.J., Nelson, C.J., Liberman, R.P., Aitchison, R.A., Lukoff, D., Elder, J.P. and Ferris, C. (1980). 'A review and critique of social skills training with schizophrenic patients', *Schizophrenia Bulletin,* **6,** 42-63.

Walster, E., Aronson, V., Abrahams, D. and Rottman, L. (1966). 'Importance of physical attractiveness in dating behaviour', *Journal of Personality and Social Psychology,* **5,** 508-516.

Watson, D. and Friend, R. (1969). 'Measurement of social-evaluative anxiety', *Journal of Consulting and Clinical Psychology,* **43,** 384-395.

Wilkinson, J. (1980). *The Assessment of Social Skill,* unpublished dissertation, University of Surrey, Guildford.

Wolpe, J. (1958). *Psychotherapy by Reciprocal Inhibition,* Stanford, Stanford University Press.

Wolpe, J. (1969). *The Practise of Behaviour Therapy,* New York, Pergamon Press.

Wolpe, J. and Lazarus, A.A. (1966). *Behaviour Therapy Techniques: A Guide to the Treatment of Neurosis,* New York, Pergamon Press.